STARTING A NEW JOB

Career Planning and Job Promotion Tactics
for Motivated New Employees

STARTING A NEW JOB

Career Planning and Job Promotion Tactics for Motivated New Employees

ROBERT MOMENT

CONTENTS

INTRODUCTION

"Success starting a new job begins
with a career plan to excel in your new position."
– Robert Moment
The Get Hired Expert

You've landed your dream job with an excellent salary and tons of benefits. You probably feel very excited and confident, as you should. However, what's next? What is your next step? Are you merely going to allow things to flow or will you make conscious efforts to ensure that you can continue to climb the ladder, setting yourself up for better positions and more benefits?

Getting a new job is much easier than keeping it. Many times, when companies downsize due to financial problems or other external factors, they start with the weakest employees whom they feel have not put their best foot forward on the job. Companies subject employees to periodic performance evaluations to analyze performance for future promotions and bonuses. You want to ensure that you are checking all the right boxes in your new role. How do you do this?

There is a great deal that can be gained from studying this book, which is aimed at providing a road map to success in your new role. The following pages will expose you to several insights and secrets that will take you from level 1 to infinity. Take a look at some of the things you will learn within these pages:

Proven Methods to Success at your New Job

This book provides you with a detailed breakdown of some proven techniques used by individuals who seek to attain success within their first 90 days of employment. It also includes a year-long career advancement success plan. To avoid overwhelming you with information, we are going to take it step by step beginning with the first 30 days before moving into 60 day, 90 day, and one year increments.

Essentials of Making Plans and Setting Goals

It's challenging to move forward if you don't have long and short term goals in place. You need to acknowledge your starting point and plan out what you intend to achieve in a specific period. It is critical to set in motion these plans when starting a new job to keep you focused and determined, enabling you to work your way up the career ladder efficiently. In these pages, you will not only learn what to do in the first 30 days but also develop a one-year career development success plan; this will enable you to get ahead in your new place of employment. In each chapter, we will look at three must-dos which are work performance goals, employee initiative goals, and personal development goals. It is integral to set these goals if you want to continue to grow and succeed.

Understanding the Importance of Building Relationships

Most dynamic companies have realized the importance of teamwork in company culture and have taken significant steps to facilitate an environment that values strong working relationships. This environment is typically built upon teambuilding events. When you walk alone, you go fast. However, when you walk with people, you go far. This cliché has never been more accurate than in the corporate setting. Here, you'll learn why you should build good working relationships with your colleagues, superiors, and business partners, and how to leverage these bonds.

The Importance of Personal Development

It is easy for employees to lose their sense of individuality when working in a company because they tend to go with the flow completely. You need to know that to move to the next stage of your career and life in general; you must invest in your knowledge; this is known as personal development. Learn what will make you stand out from other employees, what will put you on the list for the next promotion, or what will lead you to get the next juicy offer. No one wants to remain stagnant in the same role. To make a move, you must invest in yourself.

How to Get Noticed

Depending on the size of the company, it can be quite easy for employees to find themselves lost in the crowd, often with little to no acknowledgment from their supervisors even when they've kept a strong record. Thus, one of the most challenging things to learn in a new organization is the best way to get noticed. In this book, you will learn simple tactics aimed at gaining recognition from your boss, other key executives and leaders within the company. By employing these tactics, you will find that you've actively given your career a push, leaving you much better prepared to reach the next level.

However, these are not the only things that you will find within the pages of this book. You will find a wealth of information that provides specific, easy to implement strategies for succeeding in your new role and maintain an upward career trajectory. Among the topics you will find inside **Starting a New Job: Career Planning and Job Promotion Tactics for Motivated New Employees** are:

- Strategies to Succeed Faster in Your First 30-60-90 Days of Employment
- Smart Questions to Ask Your Boss in the First 90 Days
- Success Strategies to Stand Out in Your First 90 Days
- A 7 Step Plan to Getting a Promotion without Having to Ask for It
- Strategies that will Get You Promoted
- Soft Skills to Get You Ahead
- Ways to Show your Boss you are Ready for a Promotion
- 1 Year Career Advancement Success Plan
- Habits of Highly Successful Employees

Once you finish this book, you will be empowered to add several tactics and strategies to your daily efforts at work. You will have also developed a one-year success plan that you can leverage to ensure that you stay on track with your career goals. Collectively, this book provides information that will allow you to thrive in your new role, continually impressing superiors while leveraging relationships with coworkers and focusing on professional development goals.

Your game plan for success starting your new job.

Believe in yourself and your value!

CHAPTER ONE
SMART MOVES EMPLOYEES
MAKE STARTING A NEW JOB

Getting a job is no small feat considering the competition out there for the limited positions available. However, after getting the job, what next? How do you prove to the hiring manager that he made the right choice and how do you ensure this job makes a difference in your life?

Here are some smart moves you can make when starting a new role:

Prepare mentally for hard work
You are one of the best candidates for the position, don't think the story ends there because now is the time to prove that the hiring manager didn't make a mistake. Now, here is one thing you should know, the real work might be harder than the duties you saw in the job description or what the human resource officer explained. It is usually brain tasking, emotionally draining, and can sap all your energy if it takes you by surprise. Prepare your mind to expect to work hard in any job role so that you don't become overwhelmed.

When you start your new job, research and learn new skills to ensure that you carry out the tasks smoothly, learning new skills and using that knowledge to carry out your roles will not only set you apart from other colleagues, but it could also give you the chance to leave a positive impression on your manager.

Ask questions

When going to a place you've never been before, and it becomes hard to locate, what do you do? Ask questions! If there are things, you don't understand about your new job role even after doing research the next best thing is to ask your colleagues or superiors questions. Whenever you are in doubt about anything relating to the job always try to find out from those in the system.

Also, ask questions on the roles you can play to improve the organization's performance. This way, you can find out more on the company's product and services and how to use your role to enhance competition and productivity. You might even learn some secrets to a successful career by asking those who have climbed the career ladder. Don't be afraid to ask questions.

Listen and learn

You should dedicate your first day and subsequent days at work to listening and learning. Get ready to absorb, like a sponge, all the information your co-workers and manager will provide. Concentrate your efforts on understanding as they explain company procedure.

You might not be pleased with the company's procedures but rather than being critical, try to get a better understanding of why the process exists.

key people in the organization

ple have the power to decide your future within
pany. Identify them by asking your coworkers
during lunch or coffee. Also, remember to be friendly to
everyone since you are yet to know the roles they hold.

Visualize your success

Start dreaming of your big break even though you've only
begun working. Write down the long and short term
goals you want to achieve and imagine how you are going to complete them and the success it will bring.

Focus and observe the culture

Companies have both spoken and unspoken rules. The
spoken rules can be gotten easily from the company's
handbook or older employees. However, to know the
unspoken rules, you'll need to become highly observant
by watching your co-workers.

Learn the company's processes and procedures

Every company has a code of conduct they expect employees to follow. These processes and methods will be
discussed during your onboarding ceremony, but if not,
you may want to find out what they are from the human
resources officer, your direct manager or co-workers.

Stay humble

In a corporate setting, you need the help of your co-
workers and superiors to succeed. Avoid acting as if you
know it all and leave room to learn from others. When

you are humble, it's easy for people to call your attention to things you are getting wrong. It's also easy to get recommended for a promotion.

However, be careful that your humility is not perceived as timidity as that could turn you into a doormat and make opportunities pass by you. Be confident in your abilities and show that you can learn things within a short period. Don't be afraid to speak up at a meeting, team discussion or anytime you feel an injustice has occurred.

Get creative

Although it's easy to follow the company's patterns of solving specific problems, being creative and looking for better ways to solve problems makes you become a valuable employee within months of your employment. Ensure you are always thinking of ways to solve problems in your new place of work to get the attention of your supervisor or even the CEO.

Starting any new job can be an exciting, yet stressful experience. You are entering an unfamiliar environment with certain procedures or behaviors that may be drastically different than your first job. You certainly want to make a good impression, as your first impression in any job can be difficult to reverse.

Ultimately, the stakes are high. But that doesn't mean that you have an impossible task in front of you. There are a number of tactics and strategies that you can leverage to start your new job on the best foot. These tactics are universal to any organization—regardless of the size, sector, or location.

By recognizing and using these 11 Success Strategies, you can make a killer first impression during your first 90 days on the job.

11 Success Strategies for Your First 90 Days at Your New Job

1. **Listen and Learn:** This is one of the most important success strategies that you need to leverage. Especially during your first few days on the job, you must place a priority on listening and learning. This is as small as learning each of your colleagues' names to learning your organization's technology stack. On a larger scale, you must learn your company's procedures and regulations so that you can sufficiently do your job.

That said, one of the most important things to learn is your boss's communication and leadership style. Because you will be working closely with him or her, this is a task that is well worth your time. Some bosses are micromanagers and others are more passive. Some seek to empower their direct reports while others aren't afraid to take credit for your group's success. Whatever the case may be, get into your boss's head and understand how they operate. Doing this will make your life easier—both in the first 90 days and beyond.

2. **Clearly Define Success**: "Success" may sound vague or amorphous, but it is critical for you to spend some time exploring what success means at your company. One of the best ways is to ask your colleagues. Ask them directly: "How is success measured?" While you may get some varying answers, you will be in a much better position having gathered these insights from your new colleagues.

Once you have an idea of what success means, do your best to set up procedures that will get you there. If your company's idea of "success" is stellar customer service, make sure that you are delighting and surprising your customers. If it is about hitting a particular sales quota, keep that figure in mind throughout your first 90 days. Whatever the case may be, hone into that definition of success and work towards it.

3. **Set Realistic Goals**: Once you understand what success means to both you and your organization, it is important to set realistic goals. Think about where you want your career to be in the next month, six months, and one year. And then from there, work backward so that you can create micro steps toward your goals. By thinking about and setting realistic goals, you will be off to a great start.

Once you set your goals, however, make sure that you are constantly referring to them. Perhaps you can print them out and tape them to your desk. Or you can schedule a monthly check-in with yourself to determine whether or not you are on track. However you go about this, make sure that you *both* set realistic goals and take action toward those goals.

4. **Go Above and Beyond**: The first few weeks of any job offer a terrific opportunity to go above and beyond. Yes, you will want to ensure that you successfully complete your day-to-day duties. You don't want to stretch yourself too thin and give off the impression that you can't handle your regular work.

But assuming that you do have the bandwidth, don't hesitate to take on additional work as you see fit. Not only are you setting a great first impression, but it allows you additional opportunities to develop relationships with your new colleagues. And who knows? Your career may take a dramatic shift (even in those first 90 days) by going above the call of duty and taking on a project that speaks to you.

5. **Know Your Team**: Not only is it critical to know the likes and preferences of your boss, but you should have a good sense of the inner workings of your team. What are their likes and dislikes? Is there one team member that likes things done one way and another who likes them done another way? You will discover some of these traits through osmosis, but it helps to take an active, genuine interest in your team members.

Yes, there is a fine line between knowing your team and knowing *everything* about your team. But taking the time to build a profile of your team members will pay off in spades down the road. It will make your life easier.

6. **Learn and Observe the Culture**: This is a big one. While you may be able to get a sense of your organization's culture from an internship or through Glassdoor, the best way to learn about it is while you are on the job. So during your first 90 days, observe what your company's culture is *truly* like, rather than simply reading your company's mission statement or printed values. How do your colleagues treat each other? Does your organization embrace remote work or must you be in the office at a precise time? These little things matter, and the best way to get a sense of your organization's culture is by listening and observing.

7. **Identify Opportunities**: In your first 90 days, you should be on the hunt for opportunities within your organization. Whether they are opportunities within your particular group or opportunities to meet others within your company, identify and pursue them. In addition, these opportunities can be work or non-work related. Some of the best opportunities for new employees are lunches or other social events, where they can get to know their colleagues in a less stressful environment.

8. **Ask Questions**: This is something that you should be doing even beyond your 90 days, but it is especially critical when you first start your organization. Humility is

your best friend here. It is better to ask questions when you are uncertain than operate under certain assumptions that prove to be wrong. That leads to wasted time and frustrated colleagues. While you don't necessarily want to bombard your colleagues with questions, don't be afraid to speak up when you encounter ambiguities, whether they involve your day-to-day work or certain company procedures.

9. **Solicit Weekly Performance Feedback From Your Boss:** Feedback is going to be your best friend in your first 90 days. Upon starting your new job, it is in your best interest to get weekly feedback from your boss. Whether this feedback is in a pre-planned weekly meeting or in impromptu chats on Friday afternoons, you should leverage the power of direct feedback. Even if you are sensitive to criticism, this weekly feedback from your boss can be a godsend. Embrace it—even if you don't necessarily like negative things about your performance.

10. **Identify Key Actors (Employees) in the Organization:** While your boss and direct reports are key actors that you will be interacting with the most, it is in your best interest to identify other key actors in your organization. Presumably, you don't expect to stay in your current position for long. You will want more responsibility, and this often requires organizational allies to vouch for you. Yes, most of those allies will come from your group, but having key actors in other parts of your

organization can certainly help. Internal offic
can be ugly at times. However, it is impossible to avoid.
So understanding who the key actors are and starting to
build relationships with them is an important task in your
first 90 days.

11. **Set Monthly Job Performance Reviews With Your
Boss**: Finally, you will want to set up monthly job performance reviews with your boss. You don't want to
wait until the 90 days are up to complete this task. Rather, sit down with your boss and ensure that you will be
receiving frequent reviews, where your boss outlines
your strengths, weaknesses, and how you can contribute
more to the team. While you can't do much to control
the amount of effort that your boss places in your review, the simple fact of placing a regular meeting on the
books increases the chances that you will receive solid,
actionable feedback in your meetings.

Be Proactive

Using the success strategies outlined above, you will undoubtedly increase the odds of success in your first 90
days. The core theme outlining all of these success strategies is one word: *proactive*. You simply cannot expect
these success strategies to naturally happen. You need to
take control and execute.

By taking on this ownership attitude and implementing
these success strategies from the start, you will be in a
great position. From there, focus on getting to know

your colleagues, doing great work, and being a kind, respectful employee. Your efforts will be rewarded.

The first days at work can be pretty overwhelming due to all the information you'll need to absorb. However, all you need is to take one step at a time and enjoy the work environment around you. You don't need to get all the information at once, just the most important.

CHAPTER TWO
IMPORTANT QUESTIONS EVERY
EMPLOYEE STARTING A NEW JOB
SHOULD ASK THEMSELVES

As we grow and move to the next level of our lives, it's always important to know the things required of us in the near future. Most people tend to carry over what they know from their previous level to the next, but the truth is that trying this in a new job might make your co-workers and superiors view you as crude or inflexible. So, it would be best if you asked yourself questions to help determine the right things you should do at your new workplace. Here are some essential questions to get you started:

What are my responsibilities?
For every job role, there are apparent and hidden responsibilities. The obvious ones are in the job description you saw before applying or on your employment letter while the hidden ones come with the day to day activities and interactions with your manager, co-workers, and even business partners depending on your department. You are expected to carry out every responsibility that comes with your job whether explicit or hidden with no excuses. If you find out the job description and the actual roles are not related, and you are not comfortable, the best thing to do is resign.

What are the hidden roles you might be hired to do?

The secret agent

If you notice your manager is always asking what you think about other colleagues or the happenings around the office, then you might have an extra role of being the eyes and ears of your manager. This role is compromising especially if your co-workers get wind of the fact that you've been telling the boss what's meant to be employee exclusive.

Refusing to carry out this role might make your manager view you as untrustworthy. Being diplomatic and keeping the information dispersed professional is essential to avoid creating problems for you in the office. If there is something important you feel your boss should be aware of, do well to inform him but avoid unnecessary gossip about other co-workers.

The boss advocate

You might also have the task of reminding your manager or teammates the job to carry out. Alternatively, you might need to stand in for the boss in stressful situations or even taking the blame for his mistakes. When you don't carry these tasks out, you may get blamed for it which may truncate your corporate career. Prevent it from happening by learning your hidden responsibilities.

Who has the answers to success in the company?

If you've existed in this world long enough, you will agree that there are some projects you will spend time doing which will not yield results until someone shows you the ropes. It is your job to find out who knows the intricate details of how to get in the good books of your boss and other top managers, and how the department or company operates.

Observe everyone closely to know who has stayed long enough and is free to divulge such information to you. If you can get someone to do this, don't forget to ask all the necessary questions so that you don't miss anything. Appreciate the information with a simple lunch treat which could also help to build the relationship between you both.

Who can serve as your mentor?

Now you should know that the person who knows the details about the company is different from the person that should be your mentor. When seeking a mentor, it is best to pick from someone in the same department or field to help you understand your responsibilities and avoid pitfalls that could lead to job loss or keep you redundant in the company.

A mentor should be well experienced, driven and focused with an excellent track record of continuous success who can give you honest feedback about your performance as well as what you can do to improve.

How can I cooperate with co-workers?

These co-workers may or may not be part of your team, but in a corporate setting, co-workers contribute in one way or the other which could be physically, mentally, emotionally and otherwise to the success of each other. It would be best if you mapped out strategies on how to cooperate with them to achieve goals and avoid stepping on shoes that could hinder your progress.

Learn how to be a valuable member of your team and also how to help other teams succeed if you have the time to spare, but don't stretch yourself too thin that you neglect your responsibilities.

What do I need to learn to create value?

There are times you need to learn to create more value for your company and its customers. Learning on the job is excellent; however, it should be complemented with continuous professional development to become indispensable to your employer.

What are my short and long term goals?

Everyone has goals and aspirations of what they want for themselves in the future. It is essential to identify your short and long term goals of working in your new job to determine the direction of your career. Do you intend to work in the company for five years to brush up your skills for a better job elsewhere, or do you want job promotions there? It would help if you had your goals and set a plan to achieve them.

Questions are essential to help direct your thinking and improve your knowledge. Don't fail to ask questions to clarify things when you are in doubt. The answers that come from your queries will give you a strong foothold in the company.

CHAPTER THREE
FIRST 30 DAYS ON THE JOB

Depending on your terms of employment, some companies might put you on a probation period from 30-90 days to evaluate your performance before accepting you fully into their company while others will make you a full-time staff member immediately. Whatever the terms of conditions, you need to make a great impression on your superiors and co-workers in your first 30 days if you hope to succeed in your career.

In this chapter, we are going to look at the requirements to excel in your first 30 days:

The following list of tactics isn't ranked in order or terms of importance. There may be other tactics that you have used that aren't on this list. However, with that said, we encourage you to leverage any (or all) of the tactics when starting your new job. Doing this will increase your odds of success in your new gig.

11 Smart Tactics When Starting Your New Job

1. **Be On Time**: This is simple, yet powerful thing. Yes, your interviewer or human resources representative may have said that your organization is "laid back" and that people come and go as they please. We would encourage you to resist that temptation—at least in the first few weeks. If you know the time that employees typically ar-

rive at work, arrive at that time (or perhaps earlier). If you don't know, try to find out and follow the same protocol above. By being punctual, you will be starting your new job on the right foot.

2. **Mind Your Appearance**: This is similar to being punctual. It's an essential thing that is going to set you up nicely for your new gig. Instead of just throwing on outfits at the last minute, be strategic with your choices. Most likely, you will want to blend in with how your colleagues dress, but there may be some instances where you will want to be different. Ultimately, however, it is better to dress up than down in the first few weeks. Stick to a professional appearance: both in your dress and your grooming standards.

3. **Remember Names**: Some of you may find this more difficult than others. However, this is a task that you cannot ignore. As Dale Carnegie once said, "A person's name is to him or her the sweetest and most important sound in any language." While you will inevitably remember your colleagues' names with time, you should make a serious effort to learn them as quickly as possible. Perhaps create a document with names and faces of your colleagues (or access them on your company's intranet) and study them.

4. **Observe and Listen**: Upon starting your new job, there is significant value in paying close attention to how things are indeed done at your office. Take in the culture

and understand the way that your colleagues work. For instance, how are meetings run? How is the work allocated? Is there a process for sharing ideas for a particular project? What time do people typically leave work? Is remote work even a possibility? Observation and listening will be your allies in your first few weeks. By getting a better sense of your new organization, you can determine the best way to take on more significant roles in your office.

5. **Be Clear about Expectations**: Much of work is an expectations game. Your managers and bosses expect specific work from you. Customers expect certain levels of quality from you and your organization. Moreover, you expect clarity and support from your managers. When you are starting to form relationships with these groups and individuals, you must ensure that everyone is on the same page; this is especially critical with your tasks and responsibilities, as failing to do so can lead to some nasty, stressful situations. By sitting down with all relevant stakeholders and explaining what your expectations are of them (and vice versa), you can avoid confusion and disappointment down the road. While it may be awkward to have this type of conversation, we highly recommend that you do it.

6. **Plan (and Pursue) Your Goals**: Whether you took this new job because of your passion or your need for extra cash, you should take some time in your first few weeks to determine your goals. You should have both short-term and long-term goals. Think about what you

want to accomplish and who can help you on the path to your goals. From there, write them down and continually refer to them. Thinking about (and starting to pursue) your goals early in your tenure will increase the probability that you will accomplish those goals.

7. **Start New Routines**: Starting a new job is a terrific catalyst to begin building new habits. For example, one of your new rituals could be to continually seek feedback—both from colleagues on a particular project and colleagues in your office as a whole. Another routine could be joining in with organizational, social or volunteer events (even if you don't necessarily feel like it). You could also take advantage of your organization's benefits package and commit to joining a gym. Whatever the case may be, you have a unique opportunity to break through inertia and start new, productive, and healthy routines. We suggest that you don't let it go to waste.

8. **Take Care of the Procedural Tasks**: The first few weeks on the job are the perfect chance for you to eliminate every day, procedural tasks. Some of these are quite obvious. You should set up things like direct deposit (if available), select a 401(k) plan, and choose your health plan. Access all of your electronic training and finish them in your first few weeks on the job. Ultimately, you want to take care of these minor tasks when you aren't swamped with work. Unless you are entering a situation where your company immediately needs you to work on several pressing tasks, you will have the time to tick all the boxes. It would be best if you took advantage of it.

9. **<u>Start Building Genuine Relationships</u>**: This is a vital part of succeeding at any job, but it is especially important to get started in your first few weeks. Whether you are interacting with new colleagues on the job or at an after-hours social event, you should be proactive in building relationships. Take a genuine interest in your colleagues. Understand their likes and dislikes. Try to get to them beyond their role at work—regardless of whether they are "below" or "above" you on the organizational chart. Putting in the work now will not only allow you to adapt to your organization and its culture quickly, it can lay the foundation for organic mentorship opportunities in the future.

10. **<u>Seize Opportunities</u>**: The first few weeks in your new job will likely present you with some significant opportunities. Unless you have an exceptional reason, you should be biased toward taking them; this also applies to other, non-work opportunities in the office. For example, if a colleague or group of colleagues invite you to lunch your first week on the job, you should seriously consider jumping at that opportunity. If you are allowed to visit a client or go to a pitch meeting, you should do that too. Be open to serendipity. You never know what may happen.

11. **<u>However, Be Patient</u>**: You may initially think that patience and seizing opportunities are mutually exclusive. We firmly disagree with that thought. Like we stated above, it is important to have short and long-term goals

and strive toward them. However, in all likelihood, your goals aren't going to be immediately realized. It is going to take some time. For the first few weeks, it is essential to keep perspective. Recognize that you must be patient and that your first few weeks on the job may not be representative of your entire tenure at this organization. Ultimately, just work hard and keep the faith. Your patience will likely be rewarded.

Embracing Your New Adventure

Starting a new job can be exciting, yet stressful at the same time. You are going through a change (sometimes a significant difference), and change can be difficult. Some people are more adaptable than others.

Wherever you fall on the adaptability curve, there are some things that you can do to maximize this new job in front of you. By following any (or all) of the tactics listed above, you will be setting yourself up for success. Yes, the road initially may not be secure. However, by hanging tough and following some of these tactics, you can make your transition that much easier.

So work hard, get to know your colleagues, and be open to new, exciting opportunities—both inside and outside of the office. We wish you the best of luck!

3.1 How to Make a Great First Impression

There is a saying that the first impression people have about you lasts longest which is why it's necessary to make a great first impression in your new place of employment as the judgment your co-workers and superiors have about you might have a lasting impact on your career progress in the organization. Let's look at how you can make a tremendous first impression on your new job:

Dress smart

Although there have been advocacies to stop judging people by their looks, the reality is the first thing people notice is how you look. When dressing up for your first day at work, ensure you wake up early to afford you the time for proper grooming to appear professional and organized before your new work colleagues.

Find out from the human resource department if the company has a dress code or dress according to how you appeared during the interview process. Paying attention to every detail of your dress passes you off as someone organized and ready to excel in the corporate world.

Arrive early

Avoid any activity that will make you late for work as that could leave an unfavorable first impression of you. Punctuality shows dedication, determination, and organization which are essential values other members of the organization will want to see in you.

Before your first day, try commuting to work a few times to see how long it takes you to get there. If you arrive too early, you can find a coffee shop and wait there until your work day begins.

Smile
Even if you might feel nervous on your first day at work, remember to smile when meeting your co-workers and superior. Let them know you are excited to be joining their team.

Ask questions
Even if you've handled a similar role in the past, you can't possibly know it all and will need to ask questions whenever in doubt. You might want to prove to the organization that they hired the right person, but if you don't ask questions or help when necessary, you might spend more time on a job than required and may even end up doing it incorrectly.

Asking questions and following instructions will make a great impression on your colleagues. You can go an extra mile by writing down in-depth questions you wish to ask about the company the day before you start or during your orientation meetings.

Keep a positive attitude
It's your first day at work, and you may find out that some responsibilities are not the way you imagined, but rather than complain and sulk, keep your chin up and tackle all your duties with excitement. Remember to smile and be friendly with everyone you come across even the custodial staff.

Socialize with your co-workers

Extrovert, introvert, ambivert, whatever your personality type, ensure you make a conscious effort to relate with your co-workers. Prepare to respond to questions like who you are and what you were doing before joining the organization. Answering and asking questions leads to conversations which may end up in building relationships.

Embrace every opportunity to socialize either through joining the various clubs and attending events the company organizes to bring co-workers together. Never feel too proud to relate with others as it will only show you are not much of a team player.

Avoid office gossip

Remember it's a first impression day so avoid giving yourself away as someone who delights in gossip and idle talk. Stay away from people who gossip and concentrate on the job you are hired to do. If you are less busy, you can help out a colleague struggling with a task or find something worthwhile to learn.

Stay organized

Missing deadlines, meetings and having sloppy files will make you look irresponsible, unreliable and untrustworthy. Avoid these traits by making sure you do everything to keep your workplace organized. Get a filing system to keep track of your files and learn how you can keep track of meetings. Go to any length to avoid exceeding deadlines.

Remember to show appreciation

When someone has complimented your work, given a detailed explanation about a question you asked or helped you in some way to make your job easier, don't forget to say thank you or buy lunch for that person. Not everyone is kind enough to help out with your problems, so you want to ensure that they feel appreciated.

Listen and observe

Aside from asking questions, you want to ensure that you learn certain things on your own and the best way to do it is through listening and observation. Avoid trying to show off your knowledge or have strong opinions about discussions. Listen and learn about the goals your boss and other top managers have for their departments and the company. Always observe procedures and the patterns followed.

Don't stick to one colleague

This behavior is typical among introverts, trying to find the best co-worker and pairing with them all through the day. If you have this attitude, drop it and embrace everyone. Have lunch with different people so that you have the opportunity to build a rapport and understand the company's culture.

Keep learning about your company

One of the reasons the company employed you is because you took out time to research the organization. Now that you are working with them it's necessary to continue improving your knowledge by keeping up with the current news of the company and competitors, from their website, blogs, and social media platforms. Learn about the products and services to make it easier to relate to the customer base.

Stick to the rules and regulations

Every company has laid down rules and regulations they expect their employees to follow. Whatever you do, ensure that you do not break any rules especially in the first 30 days as all eyes are watching closely.

Also, follow the professional rules which are carrying out the responsibilities of your job description and those that are logically your responsibility. Avoid neglecting both of them as they go a long way in determining your career advancement.

Don't hurry home

Some companies have the culture of resuming at nine and closing by five, but the truth is that some responsibility can see you closing later than five. On your first day at work, you might want to stay longer than the closing hours even if you have nothing to do especially if your co-workers are still in the office. Don't act like you don't appreciate the environment by hurrying home.

3.2 Know and Embrace Your Team Members

You might not believe it, but the reason why you were employed is not that you had all the qualifications, but because you were a perfect fit for a team in the company. They must have seen your listening ability, problem-solving skills, and willingness to compromise which are essential attributes to getting people to work together as a team.

Now that you are part of the team, you need to contribute to its development and success. Your loyalty lies with your team first before the company as a whole. Don't try to do things that will make you look good in front of your superiors while the team the company assigned you to is underperforming.

According to Michael Jordan, one of the greatest basketball players and team leaders of all times, "Talent wins games, but teamwork and intelligence win a championship." You might have the talent, but so do others, and your new company will need you to work with the other team members they've chosen to generate revenue for the company.

How do you get to know and work with your team members with ease?

Find out about your new team
You may want to get the background information of your new unit from HR or the employee profile section of the company website or intranet; this will allow you to know more about your team members such as their skills and accomplishments. You can also use the information

to memorize employee names and faces before meeting them.

Take it a step further, discuss with your direct manager to know the behavioral issues of teammates and the strengths and weakness of each. Your manager might not see the need to divulge this information, but you can try to get it.

Be sensitive to differences

If you are going to be working with people from different backgrounds, countries, and religions, etc., you must learn to be sensitive to their differences. Have more empathy and try to read your teammates and their needs by being observant and attentive.

Attend teambuilding events

The company might decide to organize one, or a team member may feel it's better to start the weekend at the bar, whatever the case may be, attending team building events allows you an opportunity to relate with your teammates on a personal level which may help you understand them better on a corporate level.

Always create time to spend with your teammates.

Use social media platforms

The best social media platform to connect with your teammates is LinkedIn. Add them as connections and see their interests through comments and associations.

You can write about the day's work or give an acknowledgment to a deserving team member.

After LinkedIn, you might decide to add them to other social media platforms such as Facebook or Instagram, but you have to be sure they don't mind mixing work with their personal life. Also, it would be best if you were careful while interacting with your teammates on social media platforms.

Avoid saying anything negative about the company in a bid to have something to discuss with co-workers. There is the possibility that management may find out and compromise your position with the company.

Use your strengths

You have been assigned to a team to work in harmony for the company's good, and although everyone in the group has excellent talents, each has individual strengths including you. What can you do best aside from your primary responsibilities to ensure the smooth running of things on the team? Can you be a mediator between two disagreeing parties? Are you a hardcore motivator? Do you find it easy researching information? Alternatively, do you love ensuring people are well fed? Your team will quickly notice you if you can bring something new to the table.

Always find the opportunity to offer your strengths when needed. It doesn't have to be about technical duties but also general roles. Doing this will increase a sense of collaboration, cooperation, and of course, increased productivity.

Keep in mind the organization's culture which could be formal or informal when meeting your teammates to help you act appropriately and communicate effectively. Some organizations might have a defined channel of communication while others may handle things in a more relaxed manner. It would be best if you found out these things when planning to meet your new team.

Learn how to initiate small talks

Get to know your teammates on a deeper level through small discussions. Ask questions and listen attentively when the other party is talking to help you understand what else to ask. You can also build some level of trust by sharing information about you which could tempt the other person to share some too.

Ask for help

Another way to get closer to your new team is by asking them for help. Most people are happy to show new employees how things are run in the company and would immediately oblige your request which could set off a beautiful work relationship. Asking for help also indicates that you don't have a big ego and are willing to seek advice from others when you are confused or can't figure things out on your own.

Exude confidence

Everyone loves a confident person who doesn't appear cocky. Ensure that you make people see that you believe in yourself and capabilities as this will help you make valuable friendships and connections with your team-mates and even others at your place of work.

3.3 Define Success with Your Manager

Your direct manager is the key to your success in your work, always have this at the back of your mind when discussing or carrying out tasks for him. It is essential to learn tactics that will help you form a productive rela-tionship with your manager; here are some effective methods to win with him.

Define your goals

When you have been assigned a project by your manager, avoid being too eager to please and forget to secure the necessary resources to execute the plan.

Get the necessary funding or knowledge before commit-ting to the team or organizational goals so that you won't have any excuse to give as to why you didn't complete a project or do your best.

Establish how to work together

The best way to start on the right foot with your boss is through communication. It is essential to know what your manager expects from you. Does he prefer you to do all the research while he makes the presentation? Would he prefer to be fully or partially involved in projects assigned to you? Does he prefer to get involved in every decision made or does he feel employees should be able to make decisions independently?

Also, you should understand the form of communication your manager prefers. Does he prefer phone calls over emails or a physical connection over written communication? You need to know these details to avoid making mistakes that will strain your relationship.

Understand the expectations

What are the goals your manager expects you to achieve short and long term? It would help if you found out to help you get on the right track. Are there factors that will constitute success in working with him? Is there a specific way he measures success?

Some managers might have unrealistic expectations, but you must do the best you can and also communicate to him why you think some goals are unrealistic. Always strive to over-deliver in all your dealings with your manager.

Give your best performance

When you perform well at your job or any given project, your boss looks good. It shows that he is managing his team well.

Figure out what his priorities are and align them with yours. Put forth extra effort to ensure the successful execution of projects and help other team members with their tasks if you have the time to spare.

Be proactive, identify problems or potential problems and solve them before they escalate. Learn to work smart, exceed your manager's expectations.

Always endeavor to be your best, avoid giving your manager reasons to complain. By doing these things, your manager will recognize your dedication and would readily recommend you for a promotion.

Offer your help

Everyone needs help from time to time especially your boss who handles everything from their assigned teams to high profile meetings. Connect with your boss by offering to help out with things he finds difficult to manage.

Avoid asking the vague question, "How can I help?" which could mean that you are not observant enough to know in what area your direct manager needs assistance.

Offer to help your manager in specific ways. For example, there is a big meeting where he is meant to make a presentation; you can contribute your help by gathering data for it or conducting research. This effort would be much appreciated.

If there is a new project on the table, volunteer to help before being asked. While you should not try to over-burden yourself with work, determine if you can do more than your primary responsibilities.

Always remember to offer help even if your manager doesn't let you. There is a possibility you will get the chance to show your support in the future.

Give compliments

The fact that your manager is your superior does not mean he would not appreciate your compliments. Always make an effort to show him you enjoy his unique style of making decisions, managing the team, and executing projects.

These compliments will make a hiring manager feel good and think positively about you which will improve your relationship and help with your career growth.

Personal development

While trying to define success with your manager, consider your personal growth. Find out if there are any courses and programs offered by the company that will help improve your abilities.

Embrace change

If you have worked in a different company before joining this one, have it at the back of your mind that you will experience something different from your previous company. Your manager might have a different method of operation or workflow, but you need to show your dynamism by adapting.

You might even discover later that his way of doing things is more effective and productive. Do not resist change, rather be optimistic and see the bright side of things.

Make your manager look good

If you want a successful career, you want to ensure the success of your manager's job too, and this involves always putting him in a good light before his peers and superiors. Avoid criticizing him in public and take every opportunity to give him credit.

Disagreeing with your boss in public is the same thing as making them feel embarrassed which no one will take lightly. If you think they've made a mistake, tell them privately but always show unity in the public eye and you'll earn your manager's respect.

Ask smart questions

One of the most common career mistakes one can make in the corporate setting is to ask inappropriate questions. Avoid asking unnecessary questions when you can find the answers through research. There are some things your manager expects you to know and asking questions about them might make him see you as a dependent individual. Learn how to figure things out for yourself and become self-sufficient.

3.4 Solicit weekly feedback from your manager

Getting constant feedback either daily or weekly from your boss is one of the best ways to ensure success in the workplace.

Feedback helps get you on the right track and enables you to meet your manager's expectations. It also encourages frequent communication which will help in your career growth.

Employees that ask for feedback from their superiors end up becoming top performers in the workplace and experience rapid career growth through promotions and professional networks.

Most employees would love to get feedback from their manager or supervisor, but the problem is they don't know how to solicit it. Moreover, when they get feedback, they don't use it to improve their work performance.

So, how do you solicit weekly feedback from your manager? Here are a few pointers to help you:

Send an Email

The mistake some employees make when soliciting feedback from their manager is by asking for it at the wrong time or place. For example, asking for constructive criticism in the heat of a challenging project or when your boss is having lunch is the easiest way never to get feedback or probably a negative one.

Avoid asking for feedback when you run into your manager at a public place or in front of others as it might be a turn off which could cause friction between you.

It would be best if you were strategic about asking for feedback by knowing what time your boss will be free; this is when sending an email becomes essential.

When you send an email asking what time your manager will be free to give you some feedback, you are respecting the formal culture of an organization and also the fact that your boss is a busy person with whom you have to schedule a meeting.

Make sure they know the reason for the meeting which is getting feedback about your most recent performance at the workplace. If you don't get a reply immediately, wait a few days before sending a follow-up email to confirm they received your first request.

Go prepared

When your manager replies to your email and sets up a meeting ensure you go there prepared. Write questions down, so you don't forget. Moreover, talking about the issues, make them clear and specific to understand so that your boss doesn't answer an entirely different matter.

You might want to make it easier for both of you by asking a few questions that focus on areas like your performance on recent projects, and how you can expand your skill set.

Avoid bombarding your manager with questions that could be draining and cause him to avoid other important issues or even end the meeting abruptly because you exceeded your time while asking unnecessary questions.

Take notes

One of the best ways to put feedback received from your manager into use is by writing it down. Listen attentively and write down his answers to each question. This way, it's easier for you to remember and also set goals with them.

You can use your notes to outline your next course of action to improve your performance. You can take it a step further by sending your manager an email describing these actions to see if he approves.

Use feedback effectively

Your manager will feel disappointed if after giving you constructive feedback, he doesn't see any change in your performance. He might feel discouraged to provide additional input in the future unless as a warning. So how do you put the feedback you receive to work for you?

The first step is setting a goal that can be achieved within 30-60 days to ensure that you improve your performance by implementing the changes your manager identified as inadequate or not up to standard.

After exceeding the time frame you've set, share your progress with the manager by email. Let him know about your efforts and the results. This action will show that you are an employee ready to grow and will encourage your manager to give you feedback frequently.

Continue soliciting feedback

Most companies have a culture of performing a 6-month review of employees to give them feedback. However, this practice is not usually sufficient as some employees may be neck deep in the bad habits that need correction which can make it difficult to effect change.

Feedback can happen at any time, and if the company does not implement it, the employee must solicit it. Feedback can be daily, at the end of a project, weekly or monthly but not any longer than that to help improve your performance and set you up for career growth.

3.5 Understand How Your Manager's Success is measured

Aside from your job description which you should not neglect, another essential role of yours is to make your manager's job easier and make him look good in front of his superiors.

To do this successfully, you need to understand how his or her success is measured. Industry standards may differ; here are some general key measures of your manager's success:

Team's performance

Most companies measure a manager's success by looking at the overall performance of the team they lead. For example, if your manager is heading the sales team, what has been the quality of their leads? The responsibility of the team's performance lies on the manager.

Innovation

Innovation is paramount to any company that does not want to get kicked out of the market by its competitors. Companies expect managers to lead their teams to come up with innovative solutions which is why your creative ideas and actionable results are essential.

Team turnover rate

When measuring success, the company will want to know how many top-performers the manager has been able to retain. Companies need managers who can effectively coach people and help them learn new trends that will contribute to their growth. It helps employees improve their skills and helps the company stay ahead of its competitors.

Team advancement

Companies check to see if employees under the manager are getting promoted or remaining stagnant. It helps them see if managers are leaders who take out time to prepare their subordinates for more significant roles.

You need to align your interest with that of your manager to ensure his success because he is taking the glory for your performance and the blame for the lack of it.

3.6 Build relationships and network support

According to Andrew Hennigan, Networking Speaker, "Networking is a planned activity to build trust with other people to further your goals. Professional networking focuses on professional goals."

Building relationships and network support can help boost your career in ways you cannot imagine, and it's crucial to begin building one as soon as you start at your new workplace. These relationships do not have to center around your work colleagues but also clients, customers, mentors, etc.

Networking can provide you with that level of support that is impossible to get from close acquaintances. For example, if you are working in the sales department, you can quickly close a huge sales deal or make additional sales through contact with the right network.

Your network connection can get you access to private information, tacit knowledge, high-status social events, and power that will have a high impact on your organization's image. It could give you insight on how things work in another company that could be a competitor.

Your network connections can help you solve a difficult problem, give you information about the latest industry developments, provide valuable feedback, give you inside information about new opportunities, support your efforts, and teach you new things.

Career advancement is another benefit of building a quality network. When you attend professional and social events regularly, it becomes easy to get noticed while providing information and support to the people that attend those events. You can also get fresh ideas about your field or see things from a different perspective when you talk to people in your area of specialization and otherwise.

You can build confidence by pushing your insecurities aside and meeting new people. You may receive a negative reply or body language while trying to network, but frequent participation in these events will improve your self-confidence and grow your network because not everyone will reject your hand of friendship.

Building a quality network doesn't come easy because its basis is trust and a genuine relationship that could be business or personal. It's not something you can create with any random person. After establishing the network, you'll need to work hard to maintain it.

How to build a relationship and network support in the workplace

When making connections, you do not need to limit yourself to work colleagues. Your network can stretch to people with technical knowledge, consumer knowledge, business, organizational awareness, and so on. It can be people from diverse backgrounds, occupations, genders, cultures, and ages.

Network everywhere

It is easy to create a mental note of events you should network and where you shouldn't, but the truth is it's better to network everywhere you find yourself, growing various connections is more potent than similar associations.

Cultivate the habit of networking all the time to avoid missing connections that can possibly take your career to the next level. When you approach networking this way, you'll see your connections expand over time.

Where do you network?

- You can talk to colleagues who are within your team and even those in other groups during coffee or lunch time.
- Attend events, conferences, trade fairs, and other functions that bring together your colleagues or other people from different companies and businesses.
- Be active on social media platforms such as LinkedIn to establish and maintain a connection with them.
- Attend meetings with people in your professional associations.
- Attend educational programs and training classes.
- Join communities of people in your field of expertise.
- Volunteer to work on projects.

Learn to start conversations

Waiting for someone to start a conversation might never happen, and you could miss out on a valuable connection. Avoid waiting, be the ice breaker when building your network. How do you start a conversation? Introduce yourself and find out the other person's name. When making an introduction, it's essential to maintain eye contact with the person as this exudes confidence and shows you are not easily intimidated which is a trait most people appreciate. If you are going to shakes hands, ensure its firm.

You can then begin a conversation by asking "How do you do?" before asking open-ended questions that will get the other person in the mood to continue the conversation.

You can ask questions like, "Where are you from?" "Do you have a specific reason for attending this event?" "How do you like this event?" and so on.

Listen carefully to the person's reply as you could pick the next topic from it. Don't be in a hurry to ask another question; focus more on hearing as everyone needs a listening ear. Moreover, avoid sensitive matters that may make someone feel uncomfortable.

Don't get too close too soon

The prospect of gaining a new contact might feel so great that you want to give it your all to see it happen, but you might scare the other person by trying to get close too soon.

Avoid giving them the impression that you need their connection and instead pose as someone that doesn't have a hard time meeting new people.

You can give them this impression by maintaining a posture that looks like you are about to move anytime soon or exchanging pleasantries with some people as they walk past you.

Avoid lingering on a person

If you are attending an event for networking, then you should know it's unwise to talk with just one person even if you find that person exciting and you are already having a good time.

To get as many contacts as possible move around the event, have short conversations with many people, and then return at a later time to those you found their replies to be interesting. This way, you can avoid limiting yourself and make as many contacts as possible.

Make and enjoy small talk

After introducing yourself to as many people as possible and starting conversations with them, you might want to return to the people that you had the best connection with and begin small talk to get to know them on a deeper level; this is what leads to forming relationships.

While having these small talks, it is crucial to observe if the other person is comfortable. Avoid rushing to get close or making the conversation intense. Listen when they are speaking and ask questions using statements they made to show you've been listening.

Ensure you are not keeping a straight face while they are laughing as that is one of the best ways to make one uncomfortable. Find reasons to share their laughter even if you don't find anything funny. Show that you really enjoy their company and that you are not just there to add them to your list of contacts.

When referring to them, remember to call them by their first name to establish a connection. Try not to become possessive by excluding other people from your conversations.

Share stories or information that will add value and not random stories that might even sound out of place or put your listener off.

Keep a positive attitude during conversations and you will attract the attention of others who will want to interact with you, and watch your contacts multiply.

Follow up
You might have had a genuine conversation and good laughs with a few people at the event, but this doesn't mean you are friends yet. This can only happen when

you take steps to follow up after a function to continue what you've started.

You can arrange to have lunch or invite this person to a game where you can build further on the connection. This way, you can determine if they will end up being a friend or acquaintance.

It would be best if you continue maintaining contact because by doing so, their mind goes to you when they think of a particular event or industry and this could translate into real value.

For example, perhaps you work in a construction company, and they need someone to supply them with building materials or take care of a housing project, you'll be the first person that comes to mind, and this brings more wins to your company.

Note that you can build networks anywhere; it doesn't necessarily have to be at an event.

3.7 Know Your Company's Product or Service

It is essential to have an in-depth knowledge of your company's products and services as it is a critical sales skill that contributes mostly to closing deals. When you understand the various features and intricate details of the product, it is easier to talk persuasively to customers and business partners. Most times, customers complain of asking sales representatives about particular products, and they get unconvincing answers that are the result of the representative not having product knowledge.

When you know every detail about the products and services your company offers, you'll be able to answer any question the customer has with a confidence and passion that will result in trust.

Importance of product and service knowledge

An in-depth understanding of the company's products and services helps in several ways. Let's examine some of them:

Increase sales

Every company aims to sell its products and services and knowing the products helps you to outline the features and advantages in a way that convinces the customer to make a purchase.

Build customer trust

Trust prevails when there are truths and no mistakes. You can only create customer confidence when you can show or explain certain features of a product or service, and you do it with ease; this increases trust in the product and the brand as a whole.

Lasting impression

You are more likely to develop a passion for your company's products and services when you have a profound knowledge and understanding of them. The customer will notice your enthusiasm while explaining its features and will be compelled to buy.

Develops confidence

Knowledge a subject or field makes you so confident about it that even when you are called to make a two-hour speech, you won't lack words. It is the same thing that happens when you have an in-depth knowledge of your company's products and services.

Provide quality customer service

You can provide quality service to customers when you have adequate knowledge of the company's products and services. For example, someone without experience might stutter or put the customer on hold while trying to ask teammates or go through notes to get the information; this is a huge turnoff for the customer who might immediately have a change of mind except he or she has been using the product for a while.

How do you develop knowledge of your company's product and services?

The first step is ensuring that you use the products or services. There is no use working with your company if you don't appreciate their products. It merely means you do not believe in their vision or mission. If this is not the case, use their products to enable you to give honest feedback to customers. By sharing your experience with the products, the customer will be persuaded to try them.

The second step is to get acquainted with the brochures and catalogs the company has on its products or services. Study these materials regularly until you know everything in them.

You can also **gather more information from the company's webpage** where they have displayed extensive details and specifications on its product or services. Stay up to date with their online forums to know if they recently had an update or there is a sale promo.

Your **team members can provide you with more information** about the products and services if you are confused about them. Don't feel inferior about asking your teammates because you think they know everything.

Get information about your competitor's products so that you know what to say in favor of your company's products when doing a comparison. When you are not aware of your competitor's product, it is likely you don't even know what makes your product unique or stand out and this could lead your customer to think every product is the same.

You should also **pay a visit to the manufacturing site** to see how these products are produced from scratch so that you have more confidence to sell them to the customer.

You can easily break down the manufacturing process in a way that educates the consumer about the product she is about to buy. This practice will increase the buyer's trust, and might even bring a repeat purchase.

Ensure you **don't miss any sales training programs** aimed to enlighten you on the company's product and the best methods to get customers to make a purchase.

Be honest about the product's shortcomings especially if the potential customer is searching for something specific. It would be best if you directed the person to where he or she can get the products they wish to purchase while informing them of your company's products in case they need something related to it in the future.

They are more likely to come back when they need your product and services than when you deceive them into buying what they do not need.

Even if you are not in the sales department, it's essential to know your company's product. Aside from improving sales, it will also enhance branding efforts to make the products more saleable.

Know about the features such as quality, warranty (if any), delivery service, maintenance, price, strengths, limitations, a comparison value, complimenting qualities, etc.

3.8 Set realistic goals

It is normal to feel all excited about your new job and to begin setting goals such as securing a promotion next month. However, you need to know that setting goals at work are essential to keep your focus on your responsibilities and personal growth. Your goals must support the vision of the company and your career ambition. Here are some practical ways to set goals:

Set a specific and measurable goal

When setting career goals, be precise. What do you want to achieve in 30 days, 60 days, one, two three, or five years? When you set unrealistic and vague goals, it is easier to compromise and neglect those goals as time goes on.

When you know what you want, it is easy to visualize the outcome which will serve as a motivation to work hard to achieve it.

When you come up with a specific goal, make plans on how you are going to achieve it; this might include increasing your professional network, acquiring additional skills and knowledge, talking to the right people at work, connecting with your manager and so on.

Talk to your boss

One of the ways to set realistic goals is to find out what your boss expects from you so that you can align your goals with his expectations. Your success in the company largely depends on whether your superior is pleased with your performance.

Get your boss to tell you what roles you can take on at work to ease his workload and make his job easier. Ask for feedback frequently to find out how you can improve your performance.

By having these conversations, you can fine-tune your goals to the current priorities in your workplace.

Think of the big picture

You might love your workplace now, but there are chances that you might want to switch jobs in the next five years. You may also want to get promoted to a managerial position in the next 5-10 years.

How do you prepare for this eventuality? How do you accumulate success stories that will make you a suitable candidate in your next job or promotion?

Set goals to acquire the skill set you will need to achieve your goals in the future. Increase your knowledge by attending professional seminars, enrolling in educational programs or getting professional certifications.

Request support

Support could be in the form of a mentor or from your professional network; it should be someone that has your best interest in mind. They will give you the best advice to help you set realistic goals, and they will see you through the process of achievement. Listen carefully to your mentor's opinions and be humble.

Stay committed

You've set your goal, but can you stay committed to it? What can you sacrifice to achieve your goal? It is easy to set goals, but hard to stay committed while planning and working to actualize them. Lots of things can distract you or make you feel it's not worth it.

When setting your goal, be sure that it is essential and that you won't give it up for anything. If you feel it's not crucial, then set another goal; to stay committed you must believe in its importance.

If it will help you stay committed, share your goals with work colleagues or friends so that they can hold you accountable.

Keep track of your achievements

You will want to keep track of your accomplishments to enable continuous and accurate goal setting. As you move towards your goal, keep track of what you have accomplished to serve as a motivation for the things you are yet to achieve.

Keeping track of your achievements comes in handy especially when you applying for a new job or promotion. It will be to your advantage to have a list all of your wins in previous positions held because it will be easy to highlight them on your resume and make you stand out to hiring managers.

Use a Microsoft word document or excel spreadsheet to keep track of your achievements in words or numbers. Your performance at work could range from making a successful presentation to meeting deadlines, executing a tough project and so on. Don't underestimate any of it.

Make it a continuous process

Goal setting while on the new job should not be a one-off thing but a constant process where you review the goals set in the past and establish new ones. You might have had a goal to increase your professional network within a month that you achieved, but that's not where it ends. You need to set another to keep moving towards career progression and sustained performance at your workplace.

3.9 How to overcome challenges at work

Problems can come at you at any time or place which is why it's important to be prepared. Here are some smart ways to do so:

Fix it while you can

Some challenges at work can come at you subtly which could encourage ignoring or procrastination in dealing with them. For example, you might experience difficulty in using an excel spreadsheet, but because there is no need to use it in a current project, you get tempted to put off learning how to use it. Then one day, your manager comes in and informs you he wants the next presentation on an excel sheet. What do you do?

It is easy to shy away from some tasks because you find them complicated and overwhelming, but you need to know that real growth takes place where there is continuous learning. Avoid putting things off for tomorrow when you can do them today.

You might have the opportunity to get help from a colleague the first time, but what happens the next time you need help, and that person is not available? Learning new skills, and facing your challenges head-on will help accelerate your career growth and increase your confidence.

Focus on daily progress
Processes can be frustrating especially when they are long. Most times to solve particular challenges you need patience, discipline, persistence and lots of effort. You need to try lots of things to see if there would be a difference. However, as long as you are doing something about the situation, you only need to exercise some patience and trust the process.

For example, if you need certain skills to execute a project, you need to understand that it would take a while before mastering them. Similarly, if you are finding it difficult to meet your sales target remember your daily progress matters.

Whatever challenge you may encounter at work, focus on the daily progress you are making to achieve your goal rather than trying to beat the stage or thinking it's an insurmountable challenge that is impossible to solve. Keep putting forth effort to change the situation, and you'll come out victorious.

Think stress management

Stress is the next thing that comes up when you start worrying about the challenges you are facing at work. Moreover, when mental strain sits at the table of your problem, you might be a step away from total break-down which is why you need to think of a way to manage your stress.

Identify your stress relievers and incorporate them into your daily routine. It could be listening to slow music, running, yoga, long walk, sleeping, visiting friends, or even talking to someone. You need to find out what works for you and use it as recovery to the day's stress.

Talk to a friend or mentor

Now is the time to leverage your network support to an-alyze your problems with different eyes and proffer solutions. If they can't come up with one, they can at least comfort you.

If a friend has gone through that particular challenge, get them on the phone or meet up for lunch and find out how they went through their trial and was able to come out unscathed. You could get inspired by their story which will motivate you to tackle your problems.

Also, if you have a mentor, now is the time you'll want to reach out to him to walk you through the steps you can take to overcome the challenge.

You will also get the advantage of friends and mentors checking on you regularly to find out about your progress and if you are doing well. Knowing you have people that care enough to check on you will help relieve the stress too; this emphasizes the need to build relationships and support networks.

Focus on your reach
Sometimes challenges faced at work can be out of your control causing you to worry more about how you can overcome them. If it's beyond your control, there is nothing you can do but involve others like your colleagues, direct manager or another superior. Channel your energies on the things you can control.

Learn from past challenges
Challenges at work and even, in general, do not last forever, but there is a high possibility of facing them once in a while which is why you need to remember what got you into the challenge and how you got out of it, so you know what to do when faced with a fresh problem. Learn as much as you can from experience to help you when tackling a new one.

You can do this by reflecting and asking questions such as how did I get into this challenge? What have I learned from it? By thinking back, you'll be able to correctly point out the lessons you've learned which will help prevent a future occurrence.

3.10 Go above and beyond

Employees that excel at work are not those who carry out their primary responsibilities but those who walk the extra mile to ensure that their manager and company are continuously winning.

These employees climb the career ladder faster than others and get recognized daily.

If you want to make a lasting impression on your team and superiors, you must be willing to go above and beyond for them. Make a genuine impact that will make their jobs easier and you'll surely get rewarded. How do you go above and beyond for your new post? Here are some steps you should take:

Be proactive
Rather than wait for your boss to give instructions on every single assignment you can anticipate his needs and get to work immediately.

Your boss will be happy when he asks you about a project, and you respond "I'm already on it" rather than saying "I was waiting for you to give me the go ahead." How do you successfully anticipate one's needs without making the wrong decisions?

Be observant and follow the patterns. Every organization or team has a model which they adhere to and learning them is one way to get ahead in your workplace.

Think about the projects you've worked on in the past with your boss, what changes did he want? Did he request extra data? Think back on past assignments to determine what your manager will require.

Also volunteer to work on projects that are not team related bearing in mind that you are working for the organization and every unit is vital for its success.

Don't hide your ideas
There is a saying "If it's not broken, don't fix it," but this does not mean you cannot share the great thoughts you feel will help boost the company's sales or make life easier for everyone.

Even if it seems like your manager is the kind of person that delights in traditional methods of carrying out tasks, pitching your idea with a step-by-step plan will most likely capture his attention. It is easy for you to come up with excellent solutions, but when you don't have a strategy for its execution, they are dead on arrival.

Having an idea with a plan shows your manager and teammates that you've thought of the concept and made commitments to ensure it would work by researching and coming up with a plan. No one would be willing to ignore such an idea. It also shows that you are innovative, realistic and always come prepared.

Go beyond

Your duty to the company does not end with your job description. You need to go the extra mile to ensure your manager and the company looks good. Always look for ways that you can go above and beyond the existing roles and responsibilities of your position.

When you do routine things, you stay at the same level as other colleagues, but when you do extraordinary things, you become a level higher than them.

How do you go beyond for the company? Staying back after closing hours without being asked because you want to meet a deadline is one of those ways. Picking up a client's call or attending to a customer when you should be preparing to leave the office is another way.

Just like a business owner tries to do something different to set his business apart from others, employees need to understand that to set themselves apart from other colleagues; they should be doing something different.

Put feedback into action

Remember we've discussed how to solicit weekly feedback from your manager and how you should put it to work? Doing this is one way you can go above and beyond in your company.

Pay attention to your manager's observations about your projects, presentations or even relations with other colleagues and work on any loopholes he spotted. You should also pay attention to feedback from other colleagues because believe it or not; they also contribute to your success in the company.

Endeavor to improve every day at your workplace by putting every feedback to action and soliciting for more. Doing this will help you gain more trust from your colleagues, manager and other superiors.

Don't seek approval

Everyone loves a pat on the back and compliment for a job done, but this should not be the reason you go above and beyond.

Make it a part of your work culture to seek improvement by listening to feedback, acquiring a new set of skills, volunteering on projects, etc. not because you are seeking approval but because you are focused on career progression and making an impact in your new workplace. The support will surely come even when you least expect it.

3.11 Questions every new employee should ask

When starting a new job, you'll want to make sure everything is on the right track from day one. Don't get caught up in the excitement of landing a big job with a juicy salary that you ignore finding out all the details that will prolong your stay.

You need to take the opportunity of being a newcomer to ask specific questions to see if this role is a perfect fit. If you don't do it sooner, you might have some regrets later.

Here are some critical questions you might want to ask on your first day at work:

Ask your manager about the people working with you

In the corporate culture, you have to know that there is a thing called office politics where you must apply caution and diplomacy to be in the good books and avoid stepping on anyone's toes.

Ask your manager to explain the attitude of the people you'll be working with directly in the company. Is there a particular person that you should go to for advice? Are their invisible alliances or does everyone indeed work as a team? What reputation does my group have in the company?

As well as asking questions, be very observant on your first day to see things yourself and take caution. Be careful when asking questions on office politics because you may be asking the wrong person who may likely mislead you to form a conclusion when there isn't any.

Are there any weird procedures and processes?

Some things that seem reasonable to the company or the manager might be weird to you, and it's important to find them out on the first day so that you are not surprised or found doing something contrary to the status quo.

Your manager might prefer a particular means of operation which is out of the ordinary. You can find out from other colleagues about the manager's reputation. What means of communication does he prefer; phone, instant message or email? Is he a relaxed, informal type or the professionally formal type? Does he have an unusual process of doing things? Would he prefer to be copied in every email correspondence?

You wouldn't want to start your new job assuming the communication style of your manager and other procedures, so the best thing to do is ask questions.

What happened to the person in your position?

There is a possibility the person willingly resigned because of a better opportunity, but there is also the possibility of sacking which you should know. You might even find out the person got promoted to a higher position which made the position vacant.

By asking this question, you would know if your position holds any opportunities for growth or career trajectory. If you find out people do not stay long on the spot, you might want to start preparing for your exit.

Also if you find out that those who formerly occupied the position are in higher places in the company, you will want to find out the things they did and give it your best.

Time culture
Most companies stick with the traditional 9-5 while others give employees the leisure to come in when they like and work for a certain amount of time. Also, some managers keep strictly to punctuality at the office while others are all about getting the work done whenever as long as you adhere to the deadline.

Finding out what works at your new place of work earlier will give you more time to adjust especially when you are working with a team. Do they keep to 9-5 or come in whenever they please and ensure they execute the project the same day regardless of if they leave the office by 10 pm?

You won't want to be an early bird being at work by 7 am only to find out it's alright to saunter in by 10 am.

Feedback policy
Some companies conduct monthly performance reviews while others prefer to wait three or six months to do a review and tell you what they think about your performance.

You need to find out how it works to know if you have to take the responsibility upon yourself to solicit daily or weekly feedback from your direct superior to find out how you can improve your performance. If your company has a specific date for reviews, you need to mark it on your calendar and start preparing to get evaluated.

While finding out how the company evaluates and reviews your performance, you need to know their expectations of your performance too. They may have a different expectancy from what you think which is why you need to ask about it specifically.

Find out the competencies they use in measuring success during those reviews and evaluation. It could be soft skills, sales targets, customer reviews, etc.

Lunch and break protocols

Every company has a lunch break, but some companies are flexible with theirs; they allow employees to go for lunch any time they choose. Asking helps you to know how long you have for lunch if you are allowed to eat at your desk, if there is an office cafeteria, or if you need to go outside the company.

Find out the exact time employees go for lunch breaks, how many breaks are there in a day, if you can bring your food, what type of food they serve at the cafeteria, and so on.

Is there provision for help if I'm feeling overwhelmed or stressed out at work?

Work can sometimes become overwhelming especially when there are lots of projects and deadlines to meet.

In some cases, some employees experience a major breakdown when they become too stressed or overwhelmed at work.

You should find out if there is any provision for stress management at the office like a confidential hotline for employees, company therapist, gym, mentor program, etc. It is easy to assume that companies do not make provisions for such, but you'll be surprised to know they do.

Who do I go to when I have a big idea?
Aside from your primary responsibilities, you might sometimes have ideas that you feel could impact the company positively, but the challenge is how do you air this idea? Asking questions like this may reveal to you an idea portal which the company maintains and employees can use to express themselves and share thoughts.

Are there growth opportunities?
No one wants to remain stagnant in a role which is why employees are interested in whether the company can provide them with growth opportunities. You will need to find out if the company sponsors you to take courses in the company and outside.

Ask questions like, how do I get promoted? What hurdles do I have to cross? Does the company provide on the job training? What kind of projects can I expect?

Other questions employees need to ask on their first and subsequent days at work include:

- What's the company's dress code? Does it change on Fridays or maintained throughout the week?
- Is there a parking lot?
- Do I need to call in if I'm running late?
- Does the company provide me with a professional development budget?
- What are the processes for requesting leave?
- If I fall sick while working, am I free to go home or is there a sick bay?
- What will my schedule look like for the first week?
- Does the company take care of my business travel expenses or do I foot the bill?
- Do I get paid weekly or monthly?
- Can I discuss work on social media?
- Do I have monthly, quarterly or yearly performance goals?
- Do I need to attend all the company's social events? What are the mandatory or optional events?
- How many times in a week are general meetings held?

It is critical to speak with your new boss or manager within 90 days of being hired at your new company.

While you most certainly will be interacting with your boss on new projects and even at after work social events, you should take some time to sit down with your boss so that you can get to know some of the inner workings of the company. Whether this occurs in one meeting or several, asking your boss or manager for some straightforward answers to your questions can significantly help you not only adjust to your new organization but to *thrive* within your new organization.

What questions should you ask in meetings with your boss? Below are 11 smart questions that you can ask your boss in these meetings. These are not ranked in order of preference but are instead a simple collection of questions that can provide you with valuable insight when starting your new job.

11 Smart Questions to Ask Your Boss Starting a New Job in the First 90 Days

1. What are your expectations of me?

Your day-to-day work is all about expectations—regardless of the size or sector of your organization. If you and your boss aren't on the same page, it is going to make both of your jobs that much tougher. By contrast, sitting down with your boss and hearing his or her expectations of your work (and even your demeanor, if interacting with customers) will prevent disappointment or difficult conversations down the road.

2. For people like me that have recently joined the organization, where are they most likely to trip up? Also, how can I avoid those mistakes?

These are excellent questions to ask for several reasons. First, asking this question will allow you to do your job better. Compared to your predecessors who didn't ask this question, you can swiftly avoid common traps in your role. In all likelihood, your boss was forced to clean up your predecessors' messes, so asking this question also takes a potential weight off of your boss's shoulders.

Along with this, asking this question shows your humility and empathy. You show that you aren't a perfect individual and that you are willing to leverage your boss's insight to help the organization. This empathetic attitude is compelling and can be a hidden asset as an employee of your company.

3. How do those in my position advance in this organization?

Not only does this question show that you are ambitious, but it shows that you intend to spend, at the very least, the next few years with your organization. By asking this question, you can discover whether there is (or is not) a defined track record to promotion. If there is, you can understand how to best position yourself to advance along the track. If there isn't, however, you can further discuss how you can achieve your own goals of advancement at your company.

4. Tell me more about how you will be evaluating me?

While this is more of a vague question, it can provide some key insight that you can leverage before your next performance review. Are there specific metrics that will be used to judge my performance? Will I be evaluated every six or twelve months? Do I have any say in terms of how my performance will be judged? While a Human Resources representative may give you this information, you likely want to get more granular details from your boss.

5. How much autonomy am I given over my work?

Through this question, you can get to the heart of how you are experiencing your day-to-day life at your company. For instance, this question can spark a discussion over whether you can complete some of your work at home. You can obtain more clarity about how long you can take a lunch break and the times you are expected to arrive and leave the office. This question can even touch on the types of decisions you can independently make on projects.

6. If there is bad news, how would you like to hear it?

We all make mistakes. You inevitably will make them while on the job. When you do, you want to present the bad news according to your boss's preferences. He or she may want to hear the news. By contrast, they may want to listen to the news along with a solution that you have developed. Whatever it is, make sure that you are on the same page.

7. **What happened to the person before me?**

You can learn about your manager and your organization's culture. With this question, you're not trying to ambush or put your manager in an awkward spot. Instead, it is to gain more insight into whether there are certain behaviors you should avoid and your manager's leadership style. There may be some other anomalous reasons for your predecessor's departure (like office politics) that would be helpful for you to know.

8. **What's your biggest problem? Also, how can I solve it?**

In the first few weeks of your new gig, you undoubtedly will have many tasks on your plate. However, by asking this question, you can gain a better sense of what your boss's priorities are and how you can help him or her. It builds a significant amount of goodwill and can put you in your boss's good graces—especially if you can execute and help your boss solve their biggest problem.

9. **Are there any templates I can use in my day-to-day work?**

Templates are useful things. They can inform you about how work is done at your organization. They can avoid wasted time. Ultimately, they can make you less stressed. While you want to do your own, original work, you can use a template to avoid making simple, procedural mistakes with your work. So don't be afraid to ask your boss for models. They can make your life (and your boss's life) easier.

10. Whom should I meet within my first 90 days?

Quite obviously, you are going to be working closely with your boss at work. However, your boss isn't the only other person in your office. It is in your best interest to gain a better sense of your organization—especially your organization's internal politics—and one of the best ways to do this is to meet with some of those key players. While your boss may have his or her agenda, your boss should be able to make some critical introductions, which you can leverage into further introductions. You will then begin to make organic connections and will be able to understand the power dynamics within your company better.

11. When should we have more of these meetings?

Presumably, you will be asking these questions at one (or several) meetings in your first 90 days. That being said, you want to ensure that you have more one-on-one sessions with your boss. Ideally, these will be regularly, and they should be separate from regular meetings that you have in your course of work. However, by having regular, scheduled meetings, you can continue to receive feedback and continue building a close relationship with your boss.

11 Smart Questions to Ask Your Boss Starting a New Job as a Recent College Grad in Your First 90 Days of Employment

As a recent college graduate, you are undoubtedly excited about beginning your new job.

Opportunity is there for the taking.

Ultimately, you want to start your professional life on the right foot. That said, many recent college grads experience some initial shock when transitioning from academia to professional life. Working life and student life certainly aren't the same. Without quickly adjusting to life as an employee at your new organization, you will be starting your career on the wrong foot.

Therefore, when starting your new job, we encourage you to essentially interview your new boss. The interview should not be contentious or hostile. Rather, your goal is to get a better sense of your new organization, your boss's preferences and working style, and how you can thrive in your new job.

But what questions to ask? Below are 11 questions that you can ask your boss in your first 90 days of employment. While this isn't an exclusive list, we believe that the 11 questions below can provide some incredibly useful insights as you begin your new gig.

11 Smart Questions to Ask Your Boss

1. What do you expect from me?

Understanding your boss's expectations is critical—especially if this is your first job after college. In your college courses, you often receive a syllabus explaining what you will learn and how you will be evaluated. This simply isn't the case in the professional world. Therefore, you need to *directly* ask your boss about his or her expectations for you in your new role. This is an introductory question that requires some follow-up on your end. That said, it is a critical question that you should not ignore.

2. How will I receive feedback?

In school, you often receive feedback in the form of midterm and final exams. The semester is then over and you move on with your life. At work, however, feedback may not be as regular as you expect. So in your first 90 days, ask your boss about when (and in what form) you will receive feedback. Even better, schedule a regular set of meetings (perhaps weekly or biweekly) where you can receive substantive feedback.

3. Who else should I get to know?

Your boss and immediate colleagues are clearly going to be some of the most important relationships in your new organization. But having said that, there likely are other colleagues that you should get to know. Your first 90 days are a great opportunity to do just that. Assuming your boss has been working at your new organization for some time, he or she should be able to direct you to important individuals that you should meet. You never know where your career is going to take you, so the more genuine relationships you build, the better.

4. Do you expect me to be in the office at certain times of the day?

With the rise of remote working, this is an especially critical question to ask. Your boss may be strict and ask you to be in the office from 9:00 to 5:00, five days per week. By contrast, he or she may be less rigid and may allow you to work remotely—so long as your work gets done on time. Whatever the case make sure that you and your boss are on the same page.

5. Is there a defined path to getting promoted?

If you are reading this book, you are likely the type of person who doesn't want to stay in your current job forever. You crave upward mobility—maybe even your boss's job. Your first 90 days are a great opportunity to ask your boss about whether your company has a defined track for advancement. If so, you will have a roadmap that you can follow. If not, ask your boss how those in your position have been promoted. Getting this valuable information in the first 90 days will not only provide some clarity on advancement, but will avoid wasted time in the long run.

6. What are some mistakes that I should avoid?

Mistakes are inevitable at any job—especially in the first 90 days. You are going to trip up at some point. But having said that, not all mistakes are equal. By asking this question of your boss, you are increasing the odds that you avoid repeating a catastrophic mistake that your predecessor (or colleagues) have made. Not only will you build goodwill with your boss, but you will signal that you are an empathic employee who wants to make your boss's life easier.

7. At what parts of the day do you focus the most?

This may seem like an odd question, but it is another way to build goodwill with your new boss. While you want to ask your boss questions if you are unclear about an assignment, you do not want to be annoying. Along with this, there may be times of the day where your boss does not want to be bothered. The modern-day workplace is full of distractions, so you should do your best to avoid distracting your boss when he or she is most focused. Yes, emergencies happen, but you will make your boss happy by being more passive when he or she can most concentrate on their own work.

8. What is the best way to communicate with you?

Your boss has built up habits over his or her career. Some bosses prefer casual conversations in their office or the hallway. Other bosses like communicating over email or text message. Whatever the case may be, ask your boss about their preferred communication method. Also ask about how they would like to communicate in certain contexts. For instance, if your boss is facing multiple deadlines, would they prefer email over an in-person conversation? What about communicating over the weekend? Think of hypothetical scenarios that could occur at your organization and ask your boss about them. While it may seem odd to ask now, your boss will thank you later.

9. Who are the most important customers in my role?

While you may learn about important customers by osmosis, you can avoid any confusion by directly asking your boss. Even if you don't directly interact with your organization's end customers, you are still serving an "internal customer." Most likely, this is your boss, but it could also be your boss's boss. Ultimately, this is an important question because it may play a significant part in how you do your work. For instance, if you are writing a memo, you need to write the memo for a particular "audience" or "customer." Understanding who that audience is and altering your work for that audience will, undoubtedly, set you apart from others.

10. What is the biggest challenge you are facing and how can I solve it?

No matter how successful your group or organization is, your boss is currently facing at least one major challenge. It may range from finding more talent, getting a new project or initiative off the ground, or offering better customer service. Whatever the case is, ask your boss. Once you know, spend some time brainstorming on how you can help your boss solve this problem. While you may be a new employee, you certainly can provide value. Look to your strengths and leverage them when proposing solutions. Even if the problem isn't ultimately solved, asking this question (and developing potential solutions) shows your initiative and willingness to remove a major task from your boss's plate.

11. What advice would you have if you were a new employee at this organization?

Finally, this is a thought-provoking question that should deliver some interesting insights about your organization. By asking this question, you force your boss to become reflective and to deliver advice that he or she normally doesn't deliver. However your new boss answers this question, reflect on the answer. If he or she wishes that they had met more people in the first 90 days, take that answer to heart and introduce yourself to more of your colleagues. Even though your boss's answer may not necessarily be gospel, it is likely valuable information that you should leverage in your first few months at your organization.

The Beginning of Your Journey

The transition from student to professional can be jarring, yet exciting. You are entering an entirely new environment that is much more opaque than academia. In college, you know exactly what to do in order to obtain a high grade. But in the professional world, the answers aren't as clear.

Because of this, you want to leverage the experience and wisdom from your new boss. Simply put, your boss is a goldmine of information. You want to be very assertive in mining that information and using it to shine at your new job. Whether or not you get along with your boss on a personal level, you will be well served by asking these eleven questions in your first 90 days. We wish you the best of luck!

Embrace Your Inner Detective

In your first 90 days on the job, we recommend that you act like a detective. We're not saying you should be digging for dirt or information that you can leverage against someone else. Instead, we recommend that you speak with your boss to learn more about the organization and how you can best do your job.

By asking some of the questions above, you will be in an excellent position to thrive at your new organization. That said, this isn't the end of the road. You must use the information that you obtain and implement it in your day-to-day work. Yes, this sometimes can be difficult. There is a fine line between analysis and execution. However, by putting in the work and implementing your boss's insight, you can take a massive step to shine in your new role.

All it takes is an inquisitive mind, a bias for action, and the courage to implement those insights.

3.12 Work Performance Goals

Having work performance goals makes you committed to your career which reduces the chances of you becoming a job hopper. Without these goals to keep you focused, it becomes easy to lose passion for your job.

Work performance goals not only helps you stay focus; it also improves your willingness to learn and tolerate any form of stress that may come from assignments.

Moreover, you become more disciplined and concerned about the company's growth since you've included them in your performance goals.

Setting work performance goals to achieve in the first 30 days of your new job helps you perform at your best. These performance goals guide you through whatever decisions you make when relating with your superiors, colleagues and network supports. Your work performance goals also help you make decisions about your personal development.

The first step to take before setting your work performance goals is to review your job description along with your duties and responsibilities to determine what you need to achieve within the specified time.

Since you are looking to set work performance goals for the first 30 days, you may want to concentrate on shorter-term goals to allow more focus.

Ask your manager about his expectations of you aside from the job description so that you know how to set your performance goals.

Since you are starting a new job, you might have no idea where to begin in writing down your work performance goals. Here are some goals you might want to include:

- **Understand the departments in your company**
  A new employee should aim to understand the organization better, and this consists of the different departments that make up the company and how they function together to increase the company's revenue.

- **Solicit weekly for feedback from your manager**
  Ask your boss for weekly feedback on your performance and how to improve it. He should be able to give you advice on how to maintain a quality output at all times.

- **Meet your targets**
  You need to prove to management that they didn't make a mistake by hiring you; this can be done by matching your goals with department goals.

Employee Initiative Goals
Your employee initiative goals should be able to help you identify and capitalize on opportunities that will promote career growth. Here are some initiative goals to set:

- **Volunteering**

  Volunteering is the way a new employee can start showing that he or she is ready to do more than their job description.

- **Dress to succeed**

  Your dress at this stage should convey that you are happy coming to work and proud to be a member of the company.

- **Become a team player**

  Now is the time to show that you appreciate the opportunity to share common goals and aspirations with other members of the company.

Personal Development Goals

Your career cannot grow if you are not setting and achieving personal development goals. Here are some goals that will help you:

- **Improve your self-confidence**

  You need to set goals to improve on your confidence by asking your boss for feedback, ask for more responsibilities, building relationships, attend company events, etc.

- **Build relationships**

  Set goals on how to build and maintain relationships with teammates, your boss, colleagues, clients, mentor, and sponsor.

- **Wake up early**

  If you remember, one of the habits of successful people is waking up early. Set goals to be the one that wakes up early and gets to work ahead of time.

- **Work on your attitude**
  Cultivating a positive attitude helps you build and keep relationships. It can open lots of opportunity doors.

First impressions last for long if not forever. Always ensure the first impressions you make in the company are positive ones to endear you to your co-workers and manager. Team up with your teammates, embrace the company like yours, see the manager as your mentor, and always ensure you are continuously setting goals to improve your performance at work.

CHAPTER FOUR
60 DAYS ON THE JOB

Your first 30 days will likely be a whirlwind, where you are trying to remember your colleagues' names and complete all of the work assigned to you; this is all well and good. However, your next 30 days are going to be an excellent opportunity to take further responsibility and become a more valuable member of your team.

Work Performance Goals

As with your first 30 days, it is essential to continue doing excellent work for your boss. At this point, you should have a better understanding of your role, as well as your boss's likes and dislikes. While you may have made some mistakes up to this point, it's a natural part of adapting to any new job.

That said, continue to **get weekly feedback** on your work performance from your boss. You can send your boss an email or chat with him or her in the hallway. Explain that you would like to continue having weekly meetings during your first 90 days. By being proactive about feedback, you will be in a much better position to identify mistakes (some of which you may not be aware of) and take corrective action.

Beyond obtaining initial feedback, you will also want to **invest in some early wins** in your first 60 days. What do we mean by this? Essentially, what we mean is identifying and completing short, yet essential projects—ideally within your department. These early wins can show off your skills, increase your boss's confidence in you, and increase your confidence in your new role. Typically, you are assigned projects, but there isn't necessarily a rule against taking the initiative to find projects yourself. While they may not be industry-shattering projects, it is better to notch up some early wins and gain momentum than the opposite.

Work Performance Goals

Your work performance goals for the next month should be a continuation of what you started in the first 30 days. Here are some examples:

- **Build a strong relationship with a mentor**
  A mentor will advise you on steps to follow that will improve the quality of your output at work and help your career growth. Whenever you are in doubt about your career decisions, a mentor helps clear your doubts.

- **Get a sponsor**
  For career advancement, choosing a sponsor in a corporate setting should be your goal to help pave the way to your career success. You'll find out more about the benefits of having a sponsor in subsequent chapters of this book.

- **Make a list of your accomplishments**
  Don't forget to keep track of your achievements so that you will know how well you've improved

over the months. A complete list of your accomplishments will come in handy when you are trying to get a promotion or decide to look for a new job.

Employee Initiative Goals

In your first 60 days, there should be several tasks on your plate. First, ***don't let up in your campaign to meet your new colleagues***. Your brand is a real thing and is something that you cannot ignore. Unfortunately, meeting your colleagues tends to be easier in the first 30 days than the next 30 days, as everything is new and exciting. As you are getting settled into your new job, it becomes easier and easier to say "no" to that coffee or lunch meeting because of your work responsibilities.

We encourage you to embrace moderation here. While work will always be the priority, you shouldn't let up in meeting your new colleagues. The amount of effort needed will depend on the size of the organization. If you work for a smaller company, you may have already met everyone in your first 30 days. However, if you work for a larger company, don't hesitate to keep taking those meetings. Careers are fuzzy things, and you never know who is going to help you down the road. In all likelihood, it is going to be one of the people that you least expect.

Along with continuing to meet your colleagues, ***begin brainstorming ways that you can further contribute***

to the company. Doing this certainly takes effort, but it is often a requirement if you want to take on a more significant role within your organization. Within the first 60 days, you will start getting a sense of how your company can improve, whether it is through more efficient operations, better customer service, or something else. Continue observing these weaknesses and write them down. From there, reflect on how you can do your part to strengthen those weaknesses.

As a relatively new employee, you have a unique advantage in that you have a fresh pair of eyes. You can see things that long-serving employees have adjusted to or ignore. Leverage your position here. Whether you rely on solutions from the company or develop your own, start thinking about how you can pitch your ideas to management.

Employee Initiative Goals
These goals should be a continuation of your first 30 days.

- **Build relationships with co-workers**
  Extend yourself to accommodate people from other units and departments and build network support. You can achieve this by volunteering to work with them in your spare time.
- **Be innovative**
  If you have not started showing your creative skills by improving procedures and situations

around you in the first 30 days, now is an excellent time to begin.

- **Support your manager**
  Improve your relationship with your boss by aligning your interest with his. Find out how you can make his job easier and do it.

Personal Development Goals

Within your first 60 days, you should also ensure that you are meeting your personal development goals. As discussed above, some of those goals are focusing on where to direct your efforts, your personal and financial well-being.

Your first 60 days present an excellent opportunity to *attend company training sessions*. If you work at a smaller company, you may not have these opportunities. However, if you work for a mid to large size company, management may offer occasional training related to your day-to-day work. You should attend those meetings. Not only do you get a free education on specific topics that can make you a better employee, but you can continue to connect with your colleagues in a more professional setting. Also, who knows? You may come across one idea in training that you can effectively leverage on your next project.

Besides training, try to *connect with individuals in your industry*. You may sense a common theme of "networking," people are critical to your career—no matter the sector. We encourage you to get in touch with your peers at other organizations at networking events, conferences, and trade shows. Even though you may be competing with some of these individuals, it never hurts to increase your **professional network**. Compared to prior generations, today's worker is spending less time at one job. It isn't out of the question to work for a competitor in five or ten years. Because of this, don't hesitate to build those relationships. You never know how they will pay off.

Personal Development Goals

Your personal development goals at this stage should be a progression of what you started in the first month.

- **Do not procrastinate**
  If you have the terrible habit of procrastinating, you might run into a lot of problems at work especially with projects that have deadlines. Keep procrastination away by learning time management and setting up a daily schedule.

- **Be proactive**
  Learn how to make things happen around your work by taking the initiative rather than waiting for your manager to make a decision and issue a directive.

- **Be a problem solver**
  The ability to come up with a practical solution to a challenging situation is one of the best skills

you can have, and something every employee should develop.

The first month might have been to you as a baby learning how to swim, but by the second month, you should have gotten your feet on the ground. How good is your relationship with your teammates and manager? Do you know about your company's product or services? Stay focused on your goals and leave no room for distractions.

CHAPTER FIVE
90 DAYS ON THE JOB

Finally, this is the "third trimester" of your first 90 days. At this time, you may feel adjusted to your job. That said, you can't slow down now. Instead, focus on the three types of goals below so that you can finish your first 90 days on as positive a foot as possible.

Work Performance Goals

As you approach the end of your first 90 days, you will likely feel comfortable in your new role. Therefore, you **should be proactive in your day-to-day work**. While your first 30 days were predominantly about listening and observing, your focus in the last 30 should shift to making active contributions. If you are concerned about the direction of a project, speak up and (respectfully) raise your concerns. At this point, you likely have built up enough institutional capital where your expertise and opinions will be respected. If so, leverage that capital. Even if you don't have any direct reports at this time, it doesn't hurt to *act like* you already are a manager. This attitude of ownership will ease the burden on your boss and will pay dividends beyond your first 90 days.

Along with this proactive attitude, you may want to think about **pursuing a leadership role in your company**. Granted, we're not saying that you should steal decision-making authority from your boss. Instead, you should think about getting more involved in your company by pursuing an organizational committee or club. For instance, your company may have a social committee or a committee specifically for new hires. Don't be afraid to pursue leadership roles within those entities. You may hesitate at this thought if you feel like you are spread too thin. Of course, your day-to-day duties take higher priority; you don't want to sacrifice the quality of your job for a role on a board or committee. That said, if you have the bandwidth, taking on these leadership roles can be a fabulous addition to your brand. It shows the organization that you care and that you want to make your organization a better place.

Work Performance Goals

Your performance goals for the next 30 days should be a continuation of what you started in the first 60 days but with more insight for the future.

- **Stretch yourself**
  If you have not taken on additional responsibilities in a bid to go above and beyond for your company, start now. Assume responsibilities that will improve your skills as well as your value to the company.

- **Keep updating your list of accomplishments**
  You want to continue keeping track of your daily or weekly achievements; they are your investments in securing a promotion or a better job.

- **Weekly feedback**
  Continue soliciting feedback from your manager, and keep track of the changes you've made concerning negative feedback.

- **Focus on what you can control**
  Focus on the projects and assignments you have control over. If other issues are adversely affecting the company's growth, you can try coming up with a plan to alleviate them and share those ideas with your manager.

Employee Initiative Goals

One of the best things that you can do is ***be attentive to new projects that are on the horizon***. At this point, you likely know how projects are initiated and how responsibility is allocated. Use this inside knowledge to get a sense of projects that are in the pipeline.

Moreover, if you feel comfortable, step up and volunteer to work on new projects—either in a supporting role or in a leadership role. Often, it is worthwhile to take a leadership role even on an assignment that may be outside of your comfort zone. While you may make some mistakes, you will experience significant growth—both in your technical skills and your leadership skills. By working hard and doing your best work, you will likely succeed.

In addition to being attentive to these new projects, place an extra emphasis on ***avoiding mistakes that you have***

already made. Mistakes are inevitable in any job—even if you have been at a job for decades. However, what separates the average employee from the great employee is that the great employee avoids past mistakes. At this point in your new job, you have undoubtedly made mistakes (and hopefully they haven't been too serious). Now is the time to do everything possible to avoid making mistakes. You may even want to create a "mistake journal," where you can track your errors so that you don't commit them again. While you will make some mistakes in the future, you want to do everything possible to avoid making the *same* mistakes. Your boss will thank you.

Employee Initiative Goals

- **Resolve interpersonal conflict**
  Think of how you can prevent disputes and disagreements that come up when working with your team.

- **Volunteer for leadership roles**
  Volunteer for projects that will improve your leadership skill. You can also volunteer to anchor meetings or help with the hiring process.

- **Make sound decisions**
  It's your third month at the company, you've had enough time to learn about your job role and activities outside of it. Now is the time to make sound decisions that will shape your career.

- **Brainstorm ideas**
  Prove your worth and the value you add to the company by offering insightful ideas.

Personal Development Goals

Finally, you will want to focus on several personal development goals in your last trimester. One critical thing that you can do is ***track your progress toward mastering intangible skills.*** By this point, you have hopefully identified and worked on intangible skills that you want to master to advance your career. These can be more significant things like becoming a better leader or communicator, but they can also be things like bringing more energy to your company during the afternoon slump.

The end of your first 90 days is an excellent opportunity to track your progress. Ask yourself: "Am I on my way toward learning and mastering a specific skill?" If you are, congratulations! Keep up the hard work. If you aren't, be honest with yourself and determine where you are slipping up. If this task has fallen to the bottom of your to-do list, try to automate or delegate specific functions so that you can free up more time.

Your last trimester is a terrific time to ***touch base with your friends and loved ones.*** In all likelihood, you have been spending more time than usual at the office; this is often a wise decision. Starting any new job is hard, and you may need to spend extra time at the office in your first few months. However, by this time, you have likely adjusted to the work and your responsibilities. Spend some time cultivating your relationships; this can mean going out to a nice dinner with a group of friends or spending some quality weekend time with your family. While you may not necessarily want to take a vacation (depending on your workload and your company's vacation policy), you should become more present in your relationships.

No matter how you spend your time, don't ignore your relationships. Be proactive in reaching out and connecting with those who may have slipped off your radar. Ultimately, you will be a better employee by maintaining a healthy and balanced social life.

Personal Development Goals

- **Learn to manage stress**

  You've been on the job for some months now, and you may have encountered a few challenges that have introduced pressure into your life. Find out how you can manage it by trying out different stress management techniques.

- **Be a better decision maker**

  You will be making many decisions in your third month that will shape your career forever; learn how to make sound choices.

It's the third month since you started your new job, what are you doing differently? If you haven't started eyeing the next position in your company you are not ambitious enough. If you have, what are you doing to get there? It's time to review your goals and strategies to ensure career advancement.

CHAPTER SIX
HOW TO GET ON THE FAST TRACK TO CAREER SUCCESS: A 1-YEAR CAREER ADVANCEMENT SUCCESS PLAN

"I know the price of success: dedication, hard work, and an unremitting devotion to the things you want to see happen."
– Frank Lloyd Wright

Everyone wants to be at the top of their career path, but few people are willing to take steps to make it happen. One thing you should always keep in the back of your mind is that good things don't come easy.

You need to set goals and lay out a plan to help achieve them. Think of something different you can do to stand out in your workplace that will put you on a fast track for career success. Here are some basic things you can do to climb the career ladder as fast as possible:

15 Career Advancement Strategies

Moving ahead in your career can be smooth or full of hurdles depending on how well you plan and strategize. These days, the years you've spent in the company or your performance is not enough to fuel your career advancement. You need to have a strategic plan that will help direct your efforts to get your career to the height you wish. Let's take into consideration some of these proven strategic plans:

Be proactive

Look for ways to go above and beyond; provide value without being asked. Learn how to take the initiative and make decisions rather than wait for your boss to make a request, people that wait for permission to take on new assignments or tasks are only maintaining the status quo and are likely to experience slow career progress.

If you want to advance quickly in your career, you must learn how to set goals and keep moving toward them. When you are through with your assigned task, don't sit there waiting for a new one, look around and find out if there are things that need to get done and do it immediately.

However, remember to use your keen sense of judgment in differentiating projects you can take on without having to ask for permission and those you need management approval.

Be flexible

Most longtime employees in the company are usually asked to resign because they have refused to be flexible. They've continued with systems of operation that are outdated and of no business value. If you want to stay relevant in your industry, you need to keep reinventing yourself for professional growth and career advancement. Adapt to current means of communication, management styles, technology, etc.

Network

Connecting with people should be one of your performance goals as it is necessary in the corporate world. Build networks both inside and outside your company. Attend events organized by your company; attend conferences and seminars, join professional organizations, volunteer at charity organizations, etc.

Network with the right set of people in your organization especially senior mentors who can put in one or two kind words in your favor; however, avoid appearing too eager for career advancement. Let your relationship with them flow naturally.

Learn to tolerate people and focus on their positive side rather than the negative. However, if the negative side is stronger than the positive, you may want to avoid such people as they will be toxic to your career and general well-being.

Request additional responsibility

You can keep increasing your value by taking on responsibilities that are different from your job description. Doing this gives you the identity of someone passionate and dedicated to the company and its goals.

You can ask your boss for more responsibilities if you feel there is enough time to handle both your primary and extra duties. If your hands are full already, occasionally volunteer to help your manager or teammates with their projects.

Never use free time as a time for relaxation, office gossips, or walking around aimlessly. Stay busy until your shift is over, and it's time to leave.

Always communicate with your boss

By now, you should have established a bond with your boss and learned the rudiments of scheduling a meeting for a one-on-one discussion. Have a conversation with your boss occasionally informing him of your job performance and your career goals.

Ask for feedback concerning your performance and put the input you receive into action by improving your performance. Your boss should be able to tell you about your future in the company whether it looks promising or if there are things you need to do to increase your efforts.

Ask him to inform you of any opportunities that will suit your goals. If you have been a proactive employee, always protecting the interest of your boss, he will surely keep that in mind and inform you of any project or job opening within the company that matches your skillset.

Create a personal brand

Create a brand that distinguishes you from all other individuals at work. When building your brand, emphasize your strengths to enhance it. When management wants someone for a specific job, they should be able to call on you because they know what you can achieve.

Let your colleagues and superiors know you as someone dependable, that works well under pressure, takes on daring tasks, completes projects ahead of time, works with little resources, comes up with the best marketing strategies, etc.

When it comes to mode of dressing, let them know you as someone who always appears well groomed and organized. You should not only act professional but look the part too.

If you are an excellent public speaker, ensure you seize every opportunity to make speeches, be it in the company's events, seminars, presentations or conferences. Let your brand speak for you.

Learn to self-promote

When there is a need to speak up on your achievements to get certain things, you should do it rather than waiting for someone else to notice your efforts.

If you have completed a challenging professional program, let your colleagues, manager, mentor, and sponsor know about it. If you successfully executed a problematic project, inform everyone willing to listen while you provide a breakdown of how you were able to apply your skills while completing it.

Get a mentor

Your mentor should be someone with a wealth of experience who has managed to reach a certain level of success in his or her career. Most people that advance smoothly in their careers always refer back to the contribution of their mentors.

You are free to get mentors outside your work, but it is advisable to get one inside too so that it's easy to understand the experience they are relating to you. They could also serve as a sponsor speaking positively on issues concerning you and ensure that you attain higher ranks in the company.

Mentors guide you through the decisions you will be making for your career advancement. They also provide you with specific information; only people that have been privileged to work in the industry for a long time can access.

Improve your people skills

We've talked about building relationships with your teammates, co-workers, manager, mentor, and sponsor. You must improve your people skills to develop and maintain these relationships.

Learn how to be friendly, open, sociable, respect people's opinion, etc. These traits will earn you the admiration of individuals in your company as well as outside of it. Practicing this behavior will also attract opportunities to you.

Be innovative

Continue giving management reasons to keep you. If downsizing in the company should occur, why do you think the company should retain you? You want your reputation in the company to be recognized as one who thinks outside the box, contributes excellent ideas and turns them into profitable results. You should be able to inspire both new and old employees.

Observe your work environment and identify problems before taking a step further to think about creative and cost-effective methods of solving them.

Don't stop learning

People who have stopped learning are those in the grave. As long as you are breathing, you need to be open-minded and avail yourself to learning opportunities especially when you wish to advance in your career.

Keep acquiring knowledge and developing your skill set especially but not limited to those that you need to excel at your job. Learning new skills means you are preparing yourself for the next stage of career advancement. Although technical skills are essential, develop soft skills too like emotional intelligence, leadership, effective communication, and so on.

You can take your skills acquisition to a higher level by developing limited skills that only a few people can learn and master; this action is strategic especially when companies are downsizing. Ensure that you learn to the point that you become an expert in that skill and become indispensable to the company.

Aside from skills, learn about new trends such as the latest technologies to improve the ease of workflow. Also, keep up with current developments in your field of expertise. Attend seminars, conferences, professional association events, educational programs, expos, etc. to learn from others.

Participate in training programs your company offers and remember to update your resume with your newly acquired skills and the professional seminars you've attended.

Uplift others

You have to learn to carry others along be it your teammates, co-workers or employees. Everyone wants to be noticed individually, but nothing beats achieving something great as a team. Don't hesitate to volunteer to help when necessary.

Involve yourself in training new hires by being a mentor or just someone who informs them of the company's culture and key executives.

Be nice to everyone

Try to get along with everyone at work even if they don't share your interests or perspectives. Taking sides, isolating any one group of people in the corporate world will not benefit you in the long run.

Moreover, if you are not able to accept people and their behaviors, how do you hope to get promoted to the position of a manager whose duty is managing people?

Keep a smile on your face and a positive attitude. Don't take mean words thrown at you to heart, be empathetic and try to understand things from their point of view. When making decisions that will affect your teammates, be mindful that the decisions should be in their best interest.

Think of everyone as a stepping stone to success because you never know who management will ask to give them an appraisal of you.

Seek opportunities

Opportunities do not just show up or wait for you to grab them. Most times, you need to identify opportunities that are key to your success. Always keep your eyes and ears open to hear for them. Otherwise, you can create an opportunity for yourself by proposing a new project and seeing it through to completion.

Don't just choose any project without first verifying if the company will benefit from it. Identify any unexplored possibilities in your company and find out why they have not yet been explored. Are you the only one that sees these possibilities or has someone tried to find a solution and failed?

Identify the gaps you see in your corporate environment and select projects that reflect your objectives and passion. Avoid tasks that will stress you out without adding any value to your work performance.

When managing your projects, do it like a professional; avoid complaining even if you feel the budget allocated is not enough or it's more difficult than you anticipated. If you are going to work on it with your teammates, don't allow conflicts or disagreements to make a mess of an opportunity to show your superior your capability.

Create career milestones

After setting your career goals, you should create a plan in the form of turning points on how to achieve them. Set benchmarks based on your aspirations, your strengths, weaknesses, and how long it will take you to improve. Never set milestones based on others as it could lead to disappointment and frustration.

While creating career milestones, ensure that your current workplace can provide you with the tools to achieve them. If not, you might want to dust off your resume and start searching for a new job.

Write down your strengths and weaknesses and see how you can leverage them to your advantage when setting your milestones. If there is a need to improve on your faults, go for it by attending leadership programs or other programs that address your weaknesses. However, if it's something minor like being the youngest on the team, view it as a strength because you can be the most flexible and tech-savvy.

6.1 15 Things to do for your career

Here are some things you can do to ensure your path is set up for success:

Avoid taking the easy road

What sacrifice are you willing to make to get to the position you've been dreaming? It's easy to sit down, fold your arms and hope that what you wish will come to you. However, remember fortune only favors the bold.

Will you be able to put timidity aside and ask your boss for a weekly performance review or would you rather wait for the general monthly or quarterly evaluation? Are you willing to spend more hours at the office helping your boss execute projects or do you prefer packing your bags immediately at the end of your work day?

Your actions and inactions at your place of work will help determine how you progress in your career; working hard to achieve your goals is the best step to take as there is no easy road to success.

Set realistic goals

It's imperative that you set achievable goals. When you set realistic goals, you become more disciplined and focused on your target. Your goals can serve as a motivation when you face specific challenges at work and helps you overcome adversities.

Before setting your goals, you must have a clear description of what career success means to you.

Do you have the dream of becoming the CEO of a company or are you striving towards setting up your company when you've gained the experience working for others? Your definition of success matters when setting goals.

After visualizing your ultimate career goal, you need to start working towards it by breaking it down into small actionable goals to ensure that you are always making progress toward the big goal.

Schedule an informational interview with a key executive for the next position you want within the company

If you are trying to get promoted to the next position within the company, you must be willing to gather some information that will make that possible. Aside from asking your mentor or senior colleagues, you may want to schedule an interview with a key executive in your department to source for information on the things to do that can earn you that position you desire within the company.

Get a mentor within the company

It is common knowledge that most successful people have had mentors to guide them through their path to success. Getting a mentor that is within the company you are currently working for will also help fast track your career success.

The mentor you select should have years of experience and be willing to help guide you with advice that is worth more than gold.

You'll discover that it's easy to understand office politics, set work performance goals, network with the right people, go above and beyond in your workplace when you have a mentor; this is because they have gone through the same process as you, and even though some of their methods may be outdated, some of them still provide useful insight on how to steer your career in the right direction.

With the right mentor, your career will be on the right track to success. You'll find it easy to avoid mistakes that can put your job on a dead end. The problem here is finding the right mentor because most people are too busy to take time to coach up and coming employees.

It is best to know the qualities you need in a mentor and observe your superiors to know who would be a perfect match before approaching and telling them what you need. Let's examine some ways to find a mentor:

Clarity
You need to be clear about what you need from your mentor. Is it for your short or long term goals? Do you need to know the intricacies of the company? Alternatively, do you need to know how to get promoted within a short period?

If it's the latter, you will specifically need a mentor from your department because only that person would know how the department works and how performance is being measured to qualify an individual for a promotion.

Show your potential
Before going about looking for a mentor, you must be ready to show you are an ambitious person who is prepared to make sacrifices for your career. Nobody wants to waste time on someone who cannot prove their worth because it becomes a failed investment.

It may not be money, but the time a mentor spends on advice and other resources to keep you going is a kind of investment, and they need to be sure it's not going to be a waste.

Form a two-way relationship
What are you willing to do for the person you've chosen as your mentor? You can't always be on the receiving end with nothing to offer your potential adviser.

What are the things you are willing to do for your mentor to show your appreciation for the role he or she is playing in your life? Helping with their projects, watching their backs at the office, bringing lunch, etc.

You must be ready for a give and take relationship but ensure it's not anything that doesn't sit right with you or your mentor. Make sure the mentorship relationship is consistent with your core values as an individual.

Seek out a sponsor within the company

A sponsor in the corporate world is someone who wields considerable power in a company, knows your potential and is ready to help you climb the career ladder by removing obstacles along your path and speaking up on your behalf.

He or she must see your skills and abilities making a difference in many projects in the company before they accept the role of being your advocate. Here are some of the functions a sponsor can perform for an employee within the company:

- Seek out opportunities and assignments that will serve as a stepping stone to your career success.
- Include your name for any position in the company that is in line with your skills and abilities.
- Help you get promotions by speaking to top decision makers in the company.

- Convince other decision makers about your skill set when opportunities arise.
- Speak up on your behalf when you make mistakes that could quickly end your career.

Contrary to what you are thinking, a mentor is not the same thing as a sponsor; however, a mentor can also be your sponsor if that individual wields such power.

In routine settings, a mentor advises you on the steps to progress in your career while the sponsor helps you make progress by influencing major decision makers who determine your career progression in the workplace.

How do you attract sponsors within a company?
Like getting a mentor, attracting a sponsor is not an easy thing to do. You have to show that you are worth the risk and effort the sponsor is going to take when sticking his neck out for you.

If you believe that you have a positive track record along with the potential to succeed and make everyone who stood up for you proud, then reach out to your preferred sponsor and show your possibilities through your performance.

To attract sponsors, you can also try and showcase your skills and abilities when the need arises. For example, you can decide to volunteer in making a presentation for your group.

Also, interact more with your superiors such as your direct manager or those in higher positions. Show self-confidence and belief in your skills and ability as people are naturally attracted to confident people.

When talking to a potential sponsor, be prepared to walk them through your work performance since you began your new job.

He or she should be able to see great potential in you through your performance. While trying to promote your strengths, ensure you do it in such a way that you present yourself as an outstanding team player.

Be specific about your career goals with your sponsor so that he brings the right opportunities your way.

How to maintain communication with your sponsor
Ensure you stay loyal and always appreciate the fact that this person is putting their reputation on the line for you. It is vital that he or she knows that you are willing to make sacrifices for them too. If there is anything within your power to ensure your sponsor's success do it.

Always be honest with your sponsor. If you've made a mistake you feel embarrassed about, don't make another one by hiding it from your sponsor. It won't be nice if he or she has to find out from associates.

Inform your mentor about the mistakes you've made, and the lessons you've learned. Share the steps you are taking to address your inconsistencies so that if an opportunity for career advancement arises, he or she will direct it to you knowing you can handle it.

Earn trust

Your boss should be able to trust your words without giving it a second thought. Always seize opportunities to show you are a person of integrity and never be dishonest because it can generate lots of ripple effects that will tarnish your career and image.

When your manager delegates tasks to you, ensure that you complete it within the set deadline to earn his trust and establish a stronger professional relationship which would help your career progression.

Track your achievements

Most people go blank at interviews when they are asked to tell a story of when they showed leadership at their former or current place of work, and even when they do say something, it is not impressive; this leaves the interviewer with the impression that the interviewee has not had an extraordinary performance at work.

6.2 Habits of Employees that Get Promoted

"You'll never change your life until you change something you do daily. The secret of your success is found in your daily routine."
– John C. Maxwell.

Habits are things we consciously and unconsciously do every day which can make or break us. Bad habits might creep into our lives and before we even realize it becomes something hard to break. However, good habits are mostly made consciously and more often than not; always leads to success.

According to Brian Tracy, author of Habits of Successful People, "he thinks that successful people are only those with successful habits". Simply put, you are the result of what you do every day, and highly successful people have cultivated a routine that they know helps to improve the outcome of each day. What are the habits of highly successful people that keeps them at the top while they continue to aim higher, let's find out:

Start your morning early
Most successful people have early morning routines. They do not wake up by 7 am because they have to get to work by 8 am giving them time to bathe, get dressed and leave.

Highly successful people wake up earlier to incorporate some habits into their day that will help their psychological and emotional state. Example of such practices is taking out time to make their bed, meditate, workout, take deep breaths, recite positive affirmations, and eat a healthy breakfast.

These habits set them up for success during the day by clearing their heads of unnecessary tensions and worries, and also keeping them in high spirits until the close of the day. It is essential to do these things in the morning as we are often caught up with activities later in the day that it becomes difficult to incorporate them.

Never let failure define you

You must have heard this saying over and over again, and even though it sounds easy, it can be tricky getting back up after failing, but if you want to be successful, you must to do it. Failure can only last as long as you want it and not a moment longer.

Don't limit yourself from trying out new things because you are afraid of failure; that's the worst way to live your life. If you've tried to get promoted at work, and it seems like it's not working out, don't get discouraged. Keep improving your work performance and personal development so that when an opportunity presents itself, you can seize it without any doubt.

Also, if you've been called upon to make a presentation of your team's project and you mess it up, don't be too hard on yourself. Take the lessons you've learned from the failed presentation and prepare for better performance next time.

Everyone makes mistakes but the difference is some people learn from their failures, and it becomes a stepping stone to success while others dwell in it and remain low.

Have a purpose

You must have an objective before you can set a goal. What do you feel should be your purpose in life and what steps are you taking to bring it to reality? Do you want something because everyone wants it or because you know you'll have a personal satisfaction when you get it? Be individualistic; find out what makes your clock tick to enable you to live your full potential.

Working at a company not because you like their vision or culture but because they are reputable and everyone counts you lucky to get a job at such a place is not living a purpose driven life. To be successful, you must love what you do wholeheartedly. If it doesn't feel that way, you need to rethink your decision.

Take risks

Successful people take risks. Taking risks at your workplace by making the right decisions when your manager is not available to do so is another way to career success. You must be willing to take risks for your manager and the company. However, while taking these risks, ensure that they are well calculated so that you don't do anything unnecessarily.

Try stepping out of your comfort zone and make the presentations at meetings, talk to your superiors when you feel it's time for a promotion, take the initiative even when problems look impossible to solve. Don't be afraid to go the extra mile to get what you truly want.

Have confidence in your abilities

The importance of self-confidence cannot be over-emphasized, and it's one of the habits of successful people who have gotten to the highest position of the career ladder. They know their worth and are not shy to show it. They have spent years honing their skills and investing in personal development, and they are proud of the success they've made.

Did you know that even an unintelligent person can appear smart and intelligent with the right dose of confidence? Moreover, those who are full of wisdom remain relegated to the background because of their modesty? You need to understand that self-confidence is the key to moving forward in your career and life in general. Set yourself free from fear and doubt and start believing in yourself and your ability today.

Invest in yourself

Investing in your knowledge is one of the best things you can do to remain relevant in your career and life. Attending an educational seminar, enrolling in online and offline programs, and reading books, are necessary for personal development. Successful people already know this fact and are ready to invest in themselves when the opportunity presents itself.

Reading is one way to make a daily investment in improving yourself. Successful people spend at least 30 minutes a day reading books on self-help, history, and biographies. There is a wealth of knowledge to gain by reading books, just like the one you're reading right now because the author has gone above and beyond to convey vital information that will help its potential readers.

Learn how to get ahead in your career and life in general by reading books that discuss career advancement. You can even read the biographies of people who climbed the corporate ladder to the highest rung. You will undoubtedly become inspired and motivated to do more.

Spend time around inspiring people

If your circle of friends or family is made up of harmful and toxic people, your dream of becoming successful may never be actualized. Successful people surround themselves with people that inspire them to do better.

If you don't seem to have any inspirational people in your life, you can begin your search for some by volunteering for events, joining career groups, etc. to help you connect with highly motivated individuals who are full of positivity.

Here are Seven Common Habits of Promoted Employees.

1. **They Set Goals**: Promoted employees realize that promotions don't happen out of thin air. They set an overarching, long-term goal of getting promoted and then work backward to set mini goals to help get them there.

2. **They Take Action**: Goal setting is just one part of the equation. Without action, goals are just abstract things. Promoted employees actively work toward their goals—even if they are nervous, anxious, or fearful.

3. **They Embrace Leadership Roles**: Promoted employees take on leadership roles within their organizations. Whether they are leadership roles on particular projects or even on a social committee, promoted employees understand that they need to show that they can inspire and motivate their colleagues.

4. **They Are Emotionally Intelligent**: Promoted employees are emotionally intelligent. They can empathize with their colleagues and deftly handle interpersonal relationships with their coworkers.

5. **They Are Hard Workers**: This habit is hard to avoid, but luckily, it is in our control. Promoted employees are willing to put in the time and hard work at their organizations. In nearly every situation, this results in excellent work.

6. **They Are Team Players**: Promoted employees place more value on the collective than themselves. They realize that if the team does excellent work, everyone will be rewarded.

7. **They Go The Extra Mile**: Finally, promoted employees aren't satisfied with just showing up for work

and doing just enough work to stay employed. They don't hesitate to go the extra mile for their boss, team, and organization.

Keep toxic and unmotivated people at a distance so that you are not influenced by their attitude; you deserve better.

6.3 7 Steps to get a promotion without asking for one

Getting promoted at work takes you a step further to achieving your career dreams, but sometimes advancement might take longer than you had envisioned and could become frustrating. Asking for a promotion is not something you want to do because you believe your actions should speak louder than your words. However, how do you get a promotion without asking for it? Let's examine these steps:

Think career growth not status
The truth is that most employees want to get promoted to improve their situation, not their career. Focusing on learning and developing in your chosen field will get you a promotion faster than you think. Let your superiors see that knowledge is vital for you and that you'll keep on looking for opportunities to improve and advance your career growth.

Take on complex projects
Promotion to the next level means handling complicated tasks and taking on more responsibilities in addition to

your present level. Show your boss that you'll be able to handle the next level by volunteering to manage advanced projects. Handle those projects with dedication and hard work, and they'll have no option but to give you a promotion.

Consistently go above and beyond

Going above and beyond is one way to get the attention of your superiors, and when you do it often, you are setting yourself up for success at work. Keep looking for ways to add value to your team and company by doing things beyond your job description. However, don't try to make it evident that you are consciously doing it, instead make it an unconscious habit, and you'll be glad you did.

Improve your collaboration skills

Improve your teamwork skills by looking for opportunities to add value to your team and other colleagues. The higher you move up your career ladder, the more you'll be called upon to head a team. Will you be able to have a positive impact on your team members when you become a team leader? You might want to prove it to your boss now to help him decide if you are ready.

Continuous self-improvement

You should be familiar with the saying, "You only get what you give." How do you get what you give? By constant personal development. What are those things that will add value to your life and also to the company? If you don't know the answer to this question, you can start by asking your boss for suggestions before doing a personal inspection. Develop specific skills that will be important to your next career level.

Set goals
Make it a habit to set daily mini-goals that will help you get ahead in your work so that you do not spend your time focusing on unnecessary things that will not earn you a promotion.

Establish a bond with your boss
Your direct manager can be a stepping stone or a stumbling block to your career. It's safer to be in his good books so that he can help advocate for your promotion. In previous chapters, we discussed how you can build a strong rapport with your boss.

Remember his performance appraisals and make changes where necessary. You can build a stronger relationship by learning about his hobbies outside of work and using it to start a conversation in an informal setting like conferences and parties.

6.4 10 Strategies that will get you promoted

Here are some traits you need to exhibit to get management to consider you for a promotion:

Ability to delegate
Do you pride yourself as someone who takes all the responsibilities of the team, or do you work smart by

allowing team members to work on projects their way? Taking on responsibilities might seem cool, but don't make it look like your teammates are not capable of handling things on their own. One leadership trait is the ability to delegate responsibilities to the right people.

Problem-solving skills
When you can solve complex problems in any given situation within a short period, management will surely take note of you. Have a burning desire to solve problems around you both inside and outside the office.

Strong work ethic
Always stay focused on exceeding work performance goals. Learn everything about your job and ensure you are going above and beyond to make your manager's job easier.

Hard worker
Everyone admires a hardworking individual, and your boss is no different. Focus on working hard on projects assigned to you and ensuring that you don't exceed deadlines. If your boss has given you feedback on your performance, take planned steps to ensure that you put in the effort to address the weaknesses he pointed out.

Look professional
Follow your company's dress code to increase your likelihood of getting promoted. Companies care about appearances, which is why they would pay millions to keep their name from any defaming story.

If you do not always appear neatly groomed with the appropriate dress, how do you make your superiors believe you are organized and obey rules and regulations?

Be an inspiration

Companies are always looking for mentors that will train new employees to attain greater heights. Learn to share stories about your leadership experience inside and outside of your place of work. If you've not had a leadership opportunity in your workplace, there is undoubtedly something you can do outside, be it in a professional association or your living environment.

Loyalty

Show devotion to your direct manager, mentor, and sponsor. These people will inform you of promotion opportunities and even go a step further to defend your skills before executives that will decide whether you are worthy of advancement.

Emotional intelligence

Managers do not appreciate employees who complain about every little thing they are asked to do. They also do not like people who try to shift their failures onto others. If you are going to be on the list for the next promotion, you need to improve your emotional intelligence and stop complaining about every single thing.

Humility

It is easy to become proud and cocky when you feel you are more intelligent than your colleagues. Some even feel they are smarter than their boss which may be accurate but not enough to start bragging and disregarding every other person's opinion concerning issues; this is the quickest way to make enemies who will do everything possible to see you are kicked out of the organization.

Moreover, most employers are looking for humble, self-confident employees who can do a good job as well as maintain cordial relationships.

Support network

Most people who rarely miss promotion opportunities are those with mentors and sponsors. If you have not gotten a sponsor to be your advocate when a vacancy for an upper-level position pops up, then you are doing yourself a disservice.

6.5 10 Ways to show your boss you are ready for a promotion

Your boss might not know you are prepared for advancement; you may need to prove your worth. Here's how:

Showcase your talent

Being modest helps in some situations but not all and certainly not when you are trying to get a promotion without asking for one. Take on projects that give you opportunities to show your skills and when you successfully execute a task, ensure you let your manager know about it by sending an email with a breakdown of how you achieved it.

Increase your skill set

You must have gotten hired by the company because you met their requirements based on the qualities and skills you possessed at that time. Moving up in the company will require you to get more skills that will allow you to perform well in your new position.

Expand your skills while improving on those you already possess; after gaining new skills, look for opportunities to apply them in your workplace.

Request extra responsibilities

Let your boss know you are ready for a promotion by volunteering to take on additional responsibilities; this increases your value before your boss and shows your desire to help the company succeed.

Exude positivity

When we have good thoughts, our faces will beam with light, and we will spread that energy to the people around us. Always be positive about things and avoid complaining or playing the blame game because, unbeknownst to you, your boss is watching.

Solve problems alone

If you are the type of employee that runs to his boss before making every little decision, then he will feel that you are not ready to take on more significant responsibility. Show him your sense of autonomy by solving problems even during stressful situations.

Exceed expectations

There are certain expectations employers have of their employees, which is why they have work performance goals for employees. However, when you go a step further by continuously exceeding those expectations, your boss will eventually recognize the fact that you are meant to be at a higher level.

Turn grand ideas and goals into actionable results

It is not enough to think about an idea; you need to take action and ensure your idea becomes a reality. Your boss will start thinking of promoting you to a higher level where your skills can be of use.

Don't get lost in the mix

Some people get lost in the mix by maintaining their status quo, i.e., primary job description and often end up not getting noticed by their manager. Learn to put in more effort to be seen in a positive light.

Learn from your failures

When you continue making the same mistakes, you'll give your manager the impression that you don't learn. When you've made a mistake, you should not only take time to reflect but also find out the lessons you've learned from the failure. Learning from your past mistakes is one way to become the best version of yourself.

11 Best Ways to Get Promoted In Your Job (and to Show Your Boss You are Ready)

Now, here are 11 terrific ways to get promoted (and show your manager that you are ready to take on more responsibility).

1. **Take Tasks Off Your Boss's Plate**: By completing tasks that are on your boss's plate, you show that you can take on more responsibility in a higher role; this isn't the only benefit, however. You make your boss's life easier, and by doing this, you build even more goodwill with your boss.

2. **Put Forth Productive Ideas**: Generating and sharing ideas that promote growth for your group and organization is a terrific way to show your boss that you are ready for a promotion.

3. **Help Recruit New Team Members**: Finding qualified prospective candidates shows you have an eye for talent and that you foresee yourself remaining at your organization for quite some time. If you can bring in some A-list caliber talent, you can vastly increase the odds that you will be promoted.

4. **Show Your Curiosity**: If you are seen as a curious, insatiable learner, your boss will be more likely to satisfy that curiosity by giving you more responsibility in the form of a promotion.

5. **Be Known for Exemplary Customer Service**: Satisfying customers—whether they are outside your organization or are "internal customers"—is a terrific signal that you should be promoted. This skill overlaps with some other skills (namely, emotional intelligence) that signals your leadership capabilities.

6. **Constantly Learn New Skills**: Learning new skills—that are both directly related to your job and adjacent to your job—provide more tools in your toolkit. You can show off this metaphorical toolkit when seeking a promotion.

7. **Arrive Early and Stay Late**: Being a constant presence in your office shows your work ethic and increases your chances of promotion. It shows you are dedicated to the organization and that you are available to help with last minute emergencies. Sometimes, the best ability truly is availability.

8. **Make Money For Your Organization**: This is self-explanatory. If your work increases your organization's bottom line, you will get promoted. It's as simple as that.

9. **Take Ownership of Your Work**: By taking real, genuine ownership and responsibility for your work, your boss will likely reward you with even more responsibility through a promotion. It shows that you care about your work and that you want to be a key contributor to your organization.

10. **Socialize With Your Colleagues**: Whether you attend events inside or outside the office, getting to know your colleagues on a personal level builds goodwill and increases your chances of promotion. While it may be easier to keep your head down and focus on your work, socializing with colleagues will lead to strong relationships, who can put in a good word for you when you are looking to be promoted.

11. **Ensure Everything is Right at Home**: If you are facing significant personal problems at home, it will be harder to concentrate at work (and harder to get a promotion). You cannot ignore this step.

6.6 Soft skills that will get you ahead

Various factors work hand in hand when it comes to ensuring career success. You may have graduated with the best grade point average, had years of experience, etc. but if you do not have specific soft skills, you might remain stagnant in your career.

Soft skills are those essential qualities employers expect their employees to possess that will improve communication in the workplace. These soft skills increase work effectiveness and create an atmosphere where success can thrive.

Here are some of the soft skills employers recognize will get their employees ahead in their career:

Accountability

Taking responsibility for your actions and decisions will lead to career success. It's easy to make up excuses why you didn't achieve a particular goal or place the blame on someone else. However, when you dare to take responsibility for your actions even when things go wrong, you are showing the traits of a leader.

When you are accountable, it is easy to demand accountability from others, and this is what makes organizational goals achievable. Ensure that you keep agreements even when it's not convenient and accept the consequences of your actions without trying to rope in every other person around you.

Resourcefulness

What can you achieve with limited resources? Creative minds make use of the most abysmal resources to produce something extraordinary. You don't need to wait for the release of large budgets before you can execute your budget. Learn how to be a problem solver by focusing on the resources you have rather than regretting those you don't.

Empathy

Empathy and compassion are traits employers want to see in their employees as this determines how they'll relate to their colleagues and customers. If you don't have these traits, you can try developing them by volunteering for projects and events, traveling, etc. By doing these things, you are opening yourself up to people from various backgrounds, experiences, and perspectives, which in turn evokes empathy and compassion.

6.7 Keys to climbing the corporate ladder without pushing anyone off

Moving up within the organization is the main dream of employees who landed jobs they love. If possible, they will want to sit in the manager's seat within the next three months, which is almost impossible. However, at least it won't be a bad idea if they get to move to the next level now and then until they get to the CEO's seat. However, it isn't as easy as it seems.

You must have heard stories of people trapped in the same position for years without getting a chance for advancement while others who started probably a few years ago are rubbing shoulders with the top executives in the company. What do you think they did different that gave them the edge?

Before you scroll down to read the list we've prepared, take some time to think about this; if you were in the position to hand out promotions, what are the traits you would look for in your employees? Let's put aside the possibility that some supervisors might make bias decisions and promote their office pets and praise singers (which is also a strategy of its kind). Whatever comes to your mind is probably the action you need to take to start rising in your company. No thoughts? Let's help make it clear:

Step up to the challenge

The old saying that good things come to those that wait can genuinely apply to humans if we don't age. However, the reality is that the longer you wait, the closer you are to your retirement age, and the sooner you will be shown the door. You need to take action, step up, and do it now!

Go the extra mile on every assignment given to you. Ensure you get to work early, meet deadlines, take on challenging tasks, etc. If there is a unique project, everyone is dodging, step up to the challenge, and execute it.

You will not only earn respect from your colleagues, but you'll also become a source of inspiration to them, and that kind of personality does not remain at the bottom of the career ladder for too long.

Be an innovator and problem solver

Fresh ideas intrigue everyone and bringing those ideas to life earn you respect for a long time, if not for life. How do you become innovative? By solving a problem. How do you solve a problem? By being observant.

In the corporate world, there are many problems, and everyone is acting oblivious to them. Maybe they are not acting oblivious but have not taken the time to acknowledge the problem, let alone come up with a solution.

Take time to observe the corporate environment from your departmental angle or the entire organization and look for problems you can solve individually without input from others.

Having a great idea is not enough; you need to map out a plan to execute your idea. The approach, implementation, strategy, budget, and the expected result should be neatly documented in clear and easy to understand language.

Ensure you do the required research until you've become an expert and can converse on the problem and solution with ease.

Schedule a meeting with key people, like your manager, to share your idea with them. If and when your project is approved, you need to start working on it immediately to show your superiors initiative, knowledge, and dedication.

It doesn't have to be a one-time thing. Keep observing and solving problems, and in no time, you'll get noticed and highly respected.

Innovators and problem solvers within the company never go unnoticed, and they find it easy to climb the career ladder without having to pull anyone down.

Get involved

This point is somehow similar to stepping up to the challenge but entails more. If you wish to climb up the corporate ladder of your company and get to that position you envy, treat the company like it's your own. Grab every opportunity that gets you involved in the smooth running of activities in the company. Is there a leadership program available?

Try enrolling. Does your boss need volunteers to handle a particular project? Be the first volunteer. Avoid maintaining the status quo of carrying out the responsibilities in your job description and stretch yourself to accomplish more.

Doing this will earn and give you a deeper understanding of the intricacies of the company. It will help in building relationships and support networks. It will also help improve your soft and technical skills which are essential for career growth.

Aside from climbing the career ladder, these accomplishments would look good on your resume if the thought of switching jobs crosses your mind.

Be supportive

Being appreciative and supportive of your colleagues shows you are a great team player, and this is what most companies look for when hiring or promoting employees. If you are taking your career progression seriously, you must have a mentor who has taken out time to show you the ropes, give timely advice, and assist you in any way they can. So what's stopping you from doing the same for new employees and others who need it?

Be supportive of other workers; listen attentively to their problems and think of a solution together. Take on the responsibility of being a mentor to others even if you feel you are not yet prepared. It is through regular practice you become ready. Management notices employees who help others and will reward them in due course.

11 Strategies for Moving Up the Corporate Ladder (Without Pushing Anyone Off)

Here are 11 strategies you can leverage to get promoted (while not pushing your colleagues off the corporate ladder).

1. **Do Great Work**: If you are an all-star employee who shines in your day-to-day work, your boss will certainly be more likely to promote you.

2. **Make Your Intentions Known**: Tell your boss or manager that you see yourself staying at your organization and obtaining more responsibility. Sometimes, directness is needed to move up the corporate ladder—even if you get promoted months or years down the road.

3. **Network With Key Decision Makers**: You may work for a large organization that contains many deci-

sion makers. By building relationships with those decision makers, you increase the odds that they will vouch for you in the future.

4. **Build Up Your Internal Profile**: Promotions, at times, may be based on internal politics or a candidate's popularity in an office. Therefore, by increasing your profile within your organization, you make it easier for managers to pick you when they are seeking to promote current employees.

5. **Be an Intrapreneur**: By developing a project or group within your organization, you show that you have the drive, leadership skills, and initiative that can move the organization forward. These are the skills and traits that are typical of promoted employees.

6. **Make Yourself Indispensable**: If your boss recognizes that you are an indispensable member of your organization, they will be more likely to give you more responsibility and honor your ambition.

7. **Keep Learning**: Keep learning not only about your role and your desired role but about your organization and your sector. Becoming a "learning machine" will increase your chances of moving up the corporate ladder.

8. **Document Your Successes**: By writing down what you have accomplished throughout your tenure at your organization, you will have tangible evidence that shows why you should be promoted.

9. **Be Kind and Positive**: Negative and mean employees are less likely to get promoted. Embrace kindness and positivity in your day-to-day work. You will be rewarded.

10. **Follow Company Procedures**: No one wants to promote an employee that challenges or ignores company procedures. By following procedures and regulations, you show that you won't cause any unnecessary problems for your organization.

11. **Indicate Your Departure**: While this may be more of an aggressive strategy, you may increase the odds of a promotion if you signal that you are ready to leave the organization. You want to be seen, by your boss, as a driven, all-star employee that your organization would not want to lose.

Above all, have a solid understanding of the company's policies, goals, processes, and culture.

CONCLUSION

The corporate world is certainly not for the faint of heart, which means you have to toughen up and utilize all of your resources or you will find yourself missing out on great opportunities. While landing a job is a complicated process, continuing to excel in your career trajectory also takes a great deal of thought, work, and dedication.

Throughout this book, you have learned a variety of tips and strategies that will empower you to make a difference in your new job while gaining recognition and continuing to strengthen your skill set. Follow these steps to gain a foothold in your new company while following the one-year career advancement success plan to position you to attain your career dreams and goals.

Know your value! Effectively communicate your value! Demonstrate your value in the workplace!

We can't wait to hear about your career success!

ABOUT THE AUTHOR

Robert Moment is The Get Hired Expert and Interview Coach specializing in helping ambitious professionals stand out in job interviews, get hired and make more money.

Email: TheGetHiredExpert@Gmail.com

Visit HowtoAceanInterview.com for interview tips and strategies to stand out and get hired.

Printed in the USA
CPSIA information can be obtained
at www.ICGtesting.com
LVHW012002010224
770619LV00003B/601

9 781733 029605